♡Angie

"You are that rare friend you find once in a lifetime who feels more like a sister. I find myself wondering how I didn't see all along that you were an Angel among us. Your beauty was apparent, but your compassion and generosity leave a lasting effect on those who knew you. We are all more caring and accepting of others because we knew you. Your grace continues to shine bright through each of us. You may have left us here on Earth, but you will forever be present in our lives. I love you Ang."

Liz Riesen
Angie's grad school roommate & friend

"When I spent time with Angie in those last weeks, I found her strength always made me stronger, her beautiful smile warmed my heart, her outpouring of love for everyone amazed me and her strong faith gave me peace. I saw the same brave little first grade girl that came in from recess with a broken arm & a smile I will never forget."

Becky Trieber
Hospice House volunteer & former school nurse at Angie's elementary school

"I was blessed to know and care for Angie throughout her months of treatment and her final days on this side of Heaven. I saw her transform spiritually in front of my eyes. She was eager and driven to explore her faith—never afraid to ask me the hard questions, and beautifully honest in her responses. Angie taught me the importance of celebrating the every day moments, and to always carry a great purse!"

Rev. Laurel Buwalda
Chaplain

"I never truly understood how much my clients become part of my life until Anita reached out and told me that Angie had made the decision to enter hospice. We had been planning a session with the entire extended family and unfortunately that was no longer a possibility. I didn't know it until that moment but Angie had changed me. I wasn't lucky enough to know Angie before she was ill but I was certainly lucky enough to not only be impacted, but remolded as a person because of her. Which I have a sneaking suspicion is the case for many of the people lucky enough to have crossed her path.

As a photographer, it's my job to observe and document. To become completely invested if only for a brief moment in people, in their families, in the love that they have, and the love that they share. I remember leaving Angie's birthday party and thinking, 'I hope John see's the way she looks at him. I hope he knows how entirely she loves him.' I've been photographing people in love long enough to know that what they shared was rare, magical, and powerful. He looked at her the same way though. Hopelessly and entirely in love.

I overheard story after story of what a wonderful person Angie was. Her sense of humor, that infectious smile, but more importantly how much she cared about each and every one of her friends. The difference she had made in each and every one of their lives. How they were better for having known her. I learned how much she genuinely cared about people she just met (myself included).

I left that party thinking dang I wish I had known this girl in high school because my life would have been so much better. But now that I have the power of hindsight, I know that I didn't need to know her in high school for my life to be better, for me to be better. She would have taught me the exact same lessons back then as she did just a few short months ago. Because of her I more willingly and openly express the way I feel to those around me. I try extra hard to leave my judgment at the door and accept each individual as they come. Because of her, my heart is more open—it's more honest. I give more and take less. Those are all qualities she embodied. Those are all reasons she was able to impact people the way she did. Because simply put, she genuinely cared.

This doesn't just stop with Angie. It's the entire Hazel family that has changed me. Anita you and Russ have managed to raise three of the most remarkable, loving, kind, generous, and caring individuals

I can honestly say I have ever met. You and your daughters inspire me to do better, to be better, to know that I can raise my daughter to make a difference, to be the difference."

Ashley Wegh
Owner of Fly Away Photography

"I'm definitely going to treasure Angie's energy, love and overall positive outlook on EVERYTHING. Thank you [Angie] for opening up your mind, home and heart to us everyday. Thank you for approving my PTO when clearly I had only two minutes. Thank you for introducing me to quinoa (keen-wah) and wheat spaghetti (which I'm still not gonna eat lol). Thank you for telling me the BEST "Sweater-Gawd" story I've ever heard. Thank you for showing me professionalism at its best. Two years of moments. Thankful to have shared your love in this lifetime. #TeamAngie will always stay Lit!!"

Shalya Hill
Co-worker of Angie's

"Angie,

You do not know me, but I know you. Today, you helped me run twelve miles in the middle of nowhere Nebraska. Let me explain. My mother, Mary Davis, works with your sisters. She talks about them and you all of the time. She's the one who gave me the link to your blog. I've been following along ever sense. I must tell you that you are a brilliant writer / you capture raw feelings while layering the words with a sprinkle of humor, which is never easy to do–especially for someone in your situation. I deeply admire your ability to stay strong in your faith and to consciously seek the silver lining. This summer, I am running across the country for a nonprofit called the Ulman Cancer Fund for Young adults. We started in San Francisco on June 18th and we will be ending in Baltimore on August 5th. There are thirty of us, and we have each raised at a minimum $4,500 dollars for young adults impacted by cancer. Each morning, we wake up around 4 a.m. to get our eight to sixteen miles in and beat the heat. Before we begin our mileage, we have a dedication circle where we each dedicate our miles to someone impacted by cancer. Today, I ran for you. I wrote your name with a black sharpie on my left leg. Throughout the day, I derived strength from your name. Your name echoed around the confines of my skull–pushing me forward. With each stride, drop of sweat, gasp of breath, I willed that God take my strength, my energy, my health and give it to you. Tears streamed down my face amongst the sweat as I longed to trade places with you. I would in a heart beat.

I need you to know how much you inspire me–your resilient faith, optimistic personality relentless strength, and joyful soul. The person that you are makes me want to be a better person–to be more and to do more. I just want you to know that your life has already impacted far more people than you can ever imagine. I will continue to keep you and your family in my thoughts and prayers."

Caitlin Davis

"I sent a gift to Angie in hopes of brightening her day when she was very sick. In turn, Angie sent a thank you card that has been a keepsake and reminder of how she could double your gift with her words of love, and signed 'Angie' with a heart! She truly was an angel. (Angelic Angela)"

Barb Homandberg
Family friend

"When Angie was first diagnosed with cancer, I feared a life without her by my side. I had never experienced life without Angie, and it wasn't something I was prepared to endure. As she fought her battle, I saw her strength and grace in every difficult day she faced, I saw how she never lost her smile or sense of humor (she always was the funny one), and I saw the footprint she was creating by sharing her story. It didn't take me long to realize I would never have to live a life without Angie. Her memory is always with me, and as I continue to share moments with her as we did for so many years, I know she's still by my side."

Andrea Jansen
Angie's lifelong best friend

"It was a blessing to be part of her life, if only for a brief time. Her light, her soul, and her shining presence will resonate forever in my heart."

Jeanne Delzer
High school teacher of Angie

"I was one of the nurses that took care of Angie through her journey battling this awful thing we call cancer. I had the privilege of getting to know Angie on her good days and I would even say I had the privilege of taking care of her in her final days at the hospital. The hospital can be such a sad and gloomy place sometimes, especially working on a cancer floor. But not in Angie's room. Her room was filled with love, laughter, and a lot of tea packets if I remember correctly! I enjoyed my night shifts with Angie and her Mom, Anita. Angie and I talked life, boys, clothes, and careers. After she got engaged to John, we had a lot of Pinterest sessions looking at wedding themes and dresses. Angie shared her story about meeting the love of her life, her career aspirations, and love for her family. After taking care of Angie, there wasn't a shift that went by that I didn't leave the hospital with a smile on my face. Angie was one of those people that could light up a room without saying anything. She helped me learn to appreciate the things in my life, as hers was cut too short. Angie had the best people around her which is what I know helped her go so peacefully in the end. I think about Angie's Mom, Anita, everyday and think of her every time I put on my perfume as I gave her a bottle of it when Angie was in the hospital. Angie's family has made it their job to bring forth her message: Faith Over Fear. How incredible. Because of this, Angie's memory and message will live on to help others."

Molly Buche
Nurse who cared for Angie

FAITH OVER FEAR
Walking Angie Home

faith / fear †

FAITH OVER FEAR
Walking Angie Home

faith / fear †

ANGIE HAZEL

JESSY PAULSON CASSY DEBRUIN

ANITA HAZEL JOHN KOLBACH

THRONE
PUBLISHING GROUP

ISBN: 978-1-949550-11-5
Ebook ISBN: 978-1-949550-12-2

Printed in the United States of America.

Although the author and publisher have made every effort to ensure that the information and advice in this book was correct and accurate at press time, the author and publisher do not assume and hereby disclaim any liability to any party for any loss, damage, or disruption caused from acting upon the information in this book or by errors or omissions, whether such errors or omissions result from negligence, accident, or any other cause.

For quantity orders, speaking engagements or inquiries please contact:
Jessy Paulson
Email: jessyhazel@hotmail.com

DEDICATION

This book is dedicated to Angie, who taught us the meaning of having Faith Over Fear, and not letting the devil steal our peace, to God who held us tight and lined our path with "God Things" along the way, and to everyone who walked with us in support. We are eternally grateful for all we have been given. May Angie's message be spread as wide as God intends.

She was powerful,
not because she wasn't scared,
but because she went on so strongly,
despite the fear.

-Atticus

CONTENTS

CONTENTS

FOREWORD

We are each in control of our day ... or are we? How do you find yourself when suddenly the "what if's" become your new day?

As an oncology (cancer) nurse for over thirty years, certain patients remain in my heart. There is one who taught me more about faith in the presence of the unknown—more than I can ever teach anyone. She was my neighbor, who is the same age as my own children, and who you will get to know as you dive into this book, Angela (Angie) Hazel.

My day came to a halt when Angie's father, Russ, had called me at work, "Angie is sick, she is real sick...and we can't get answers." A parent's worst nightmare. A father trying to gain control of something that none of us could even grasp. Being six hours away, not knowing the medical system and hearing Angie's voice through the phone that she was in pain, she was struggling to catch her breath and her need for answers for medical care were happening at a snail pace.

These are our neighbors, our families have lived across the section from each other for many years. This family was the type of friends that would drop everything to be at your side. Russ and my husband had worked together for years at a local energy refinery. Our lives had also been sewn together several years earlier when another family member had leukemia and I was able to help find medical care that would eventually lead to a cure.

Angie was so young, she had her entire life in front of her. As a young girl, her contagious smile would capture the room and we would all be laughing. As a dietitian, she herself connected with patients and co-workers. They would later come to rally at her side.

I took down all the information that I could get. I cornered my hematology physician friend. He knew the family and had directed the care for Angie's uncle's cure. Her age, symptoms, and increased weakness had him very concerned. He suggested several tests that I communicated back to Angie's father. A biopsy was done-but we could not get the results-they were slow in processing....and every minute, Angie was having increased pain, increased trouble breathing-she was now on oxygen...in less than 24 hours she was becoming unable to do simple things. Each report from Angie's parents gave additional clues as to how quickly this disease-whatever it was, was imprisoning Angie. I spoke to Angie, tears rolled down my face in silence as I listened to her describe how terrible she was feeling. It was coming up on a weekend, the family made the decision to bring her home. Secretly, I was praying and praising God for that decision-as now I really could help her find a physician that could give her the best care possible.

After another phone call to my physician friend, he moved his schedule and made arrangements to see Angie on Monday morning-first thing. "Thank you Lord", He was pulling strings where normally it would be days to be seen. God was in the midst-he was hearing our prayers.

Towards the middle of the day, I found Angie laying in a bed, oxygen mask on-recovering from being poked and multiple tests. Through all the struggles of the day, her contagious smile came through the mask-"thank you". I had not done anything-I wanted to hug her as my own child and take this all away.

Angie was ready to fight as she began her hospital stay that night with us on the oncology unit. My physician friend came to my side, pulled me away and honestly stated "this is not good. I am not the right physician for this, but I know who is and have already consulted him." Again Thank you Lord....we were moving forward.

This is Angie's story. Her walk in faith through an unknown disease with no reason of "Why"!

By Lola Twedt

The Lord is my light
and my salvation—so
why should I be
afraid?

Psalm 27:1

♡Angie

INTRODUCTION

This book is about Angie and her undeniable wit, kindness, strength, and faith. But this book is about more than just her battle through cancer. It is about how one person can impact countless others. It is about the importance of family and having resilience amidst the toughest times in life. Most of all, it is about having Faith Over Fear.

ANGIE

April 5, 1991, on an unseasonably warm 90-degree day in South Dakota, Angela Marcy Hazel was born. The second beautiful rainbow baby, Angie was the perfect addition to complete our family of five. As Angie grew, it was evident very quickly that she was full of life and love. Ang was the kind of kid that kept everyone on their toes. She awoke most days at 5 a.m., bouncing out of bed, ready to go. Everything with Angie was full force. When she sang, it was at the top of her lungs–usually a made-up song about randomness. When she played, she was so excited that she would knock over the Barbie houses carefully set up by her older sisters. And when she napped, she slept hard for hours at a time. From the time she was little, Angie did everything with her whole heart and soul into it.

As she grew, it was clear Angie loved people and they loved her back. She made friends easily with her approachable personality, wittiness, and genuine smile. Her closest friends got to be part of the full "Angie Experience" her family was accustomed to. Weekends were often spent having sleepovers where Ang and her friends would perform songs and plays that were carefully choreographed with costumes and all. Many times, these performances were videotaped by another family member or friend. Angie was a "YouTuber" long before it was a thing.

In high school, Ang's friend list continued to grow as she met new people in the many clubs and groups she was involved in. She was homecoming queen in our small town high school and moved on to college at South Dakota State University. Her many jobs working with food and healthcare throughout high school and college paved the way for her dream career as a dietitian. After SDSU she went on to the University of Missouri in Springfield for graduate school. She had big goals and dreams and she did everything with the same passion and enthusiasm she had as a kid. As a dietitian, Angie wanted to improve the quality of life for people through simple changes in diet. She understood the importance of good nutrition, especially for mothers and children, and she found her career in the downtown WIC clinic in Kansas City.

In Kansas City, she built her home with her long-time boyfriend, John, and their goldendoodle, Kona. She filled her days focused on her work, and her time off was focused on her family and friends. They traveled the country together, reconnecting often with their large circle of friends, which became like extended family. Angie's passions melted into one another. She often offered food suggestions to make her family and friends healthier, she was active with her dog, and her life was constantly on the go.

Above all, Angie adored her people, her God-given family, and those who entered her life as friends and became like family. She talked to her Mom daily and her sisters and Dad often. Her best friends in elementary school continued to be her closest friends as an adult, even as her circle grew.

Conversations with Ang always felt intimate and she remembered details most people would forget in an instant. She treated her nieces and nephews like her own children. Each visit, they would all run and jump on her, anxious to tell her their stories or show her their latest toy or skill. Ang had a way of making everyone feel special, especially the kids by giving them the time and attention they craved from her, at least for the first few hours of every visit, until they wore her out and she was ready for one of her famous naps. She made a point to be present in the day to day, even if she wasn't physically here. A continuous group text about the randomness of the day and a FaceTime here and there kept her in the loop, even from a distance.

Often when Angie was little and had to clean her room, she would declare she was done and the room appeared to be perfectly in order. But when you entered the room and really looked around, it was clear Angie had shoved all her stuff into the space between her bed and the wall. That was Ang. She was always good at putting everything together so that it seemed to be well in order–even perfect. But when she let you into her life, it was clear things weren't as perfect as they appeared on the outside. Instead, you found out things were a beautiful mess, which is so much better. She was relatable, she was kind, she didn't bat an eye if things were a disaster. Instead, she did what she could to help you out, because she herself was a beautiful mess as well. She was full of grace, and she was human in every sense of the word.

CHAPTER 1

If Only This Had Started With A Cat Scratch

CARINGBRIDGE POST
by Angela Hazel, March 12, 2017

Brace yourselves for a real romantic story here, people. Everything started with a fatty lump of misdirected breast tissue in my armpit. If anyone remembers, about 8 years ago I had another lipoma in my right armpit, which was promptly removed and never to be spoken of again (because trust me, it was gross). The initial lipoma I had in my right armpit was benign and the breast surgeon that handled my case then never even uttered the word "cancer". When I noticed the fatty tissue growing under my left armpit, all I could selfishly think was, "Man, I need to get this removed before I go on vacation in April!"

The real trouble started about 6 weeks ago. After starting a new yoga class, I began to have pain and numbness down my left arm when I slept on my side. I thought maybe I overworked that area and took 2 weeks off of my class to see if that helped with the pain. It didn't. I scheduled an appointment with my primary care doctor and in the meantime, visited my chiropractor. I figured the fatty tissue in the left armpit was building up and affecting the nerves around it, or I might even have to have a cyst removed (anyone watch Dr. Pimple Popper on YouTube?).

Fast forward a couple weeks, and things changed dramatically. I went from having some arm pain, to showing significant weight loss, complaining of tiredness all the time, experienced loss of appetite, and basically struggling to get through the workday. A few days before my scheduled doctor appointment, I developed an incredibly stubborn dry cough and a sharp pain when I drew in a deep breath. At my doctor appointment, it was concluded that I had enlarged lymph nodes in my left axillary region (less disgusting way to talk about my armpit), enlarged lymph nodes on my neck, and possibly a virus due to the dry cough. My doctor ran some blood tests (CBC and thyroid function) and set me up with an appointment for an ultrasound to figure out why these lymph nodes blew up like balloons.

I visited a breast surgeon's office to consult about the ultrasound and learned there were three feisty lymph nodes that were around 4 times bigger than the well-behaved lymph nodes surrounding them. The doctor originally planned to do a needle biopsy, but as more information came back to my primary doctor regarding other test results, they realized that a full surgical excision would be the best option as it could be one of four results: infection, inflammation, a non-cancerous tumor or a cancerous tumor.

The next day, I was set up for a chest x-ray to check out my cough and a vampire of a lab tech drew out at least half of the blood in my body for various testing...no joke. They took SO. MUCH. BLOOD. They began by looking at liver function tests and infectious diseases. I was asked 100 times if I had a cat at home or had played with the cat because I think everyone was crossing their fingers that I simply had cat scratch disease (it's a real thing, look it up!) rather than the alternative options. Most of the blood work did not come back until the following week, but I did find out that same day that my liver function was decreased, my white cell count was elevated, my thyroid was fine, and that I had "innumerable ill-defined nodular opacities bilaterally with a lower lung zone predominance" and that the primary differential considerations include neoplastic process (tumor). So yes, Friday was full of great news and no real answers. The doctor wanted me to follow up on Monday for a CT scan and a biopsy on Tuesday.

At this point, my family was very involved in the testing procedures I underwent, and my Mom and Dad felt they needed to drive down to see me ASAP. On Friday, I felt well enough considering, and was taking Tylenol for severe lower back pain because NSAIDS were banned until after my surgery. Saturday led to more back pain, resulting in calling the on-call doctor to see what else I could safely take for pain management until Tuesday. Sunday was the brutal turning point. I was taking the maximum amount of Tylenol possible to combat the bone pain, and I was still breaking down in pain and tears, immobile, 2 hours before I could even think of taking my next dose of medicine. The shortness of breath when the pain was so high led us to the emergency room late that evening.

While the cool 45-minute drive in agonizing pain wasn't fun, the morphine made everything better for a moment. Upon arrival, they immediately got me started on pain medications and did an EKG to be sure I wasn't hiding a blood clot in my lungs. Once that was ruled out, I was wheeled off to do my CT scan of the chest, abdomen and pelvis. The doctor returned a while later to tell us that there were again more "scary spots" on my spine and pelvis (hence the incredible back pain), in addition to the ones on my lungs. The initial report from radiology led us to believe they weren't too worried with the spots on my lungs, suggesting it might just be fungal pneumonia or TB, but also straight up said, "the multiple lucent lesions on the spine likely represent metastatic disease." The ED doctor knew this, obviously, but we didn't at this point. Everyone was still throwing around the word "infection" and as much as I dislike cats, I sure hoped that all I had was some crazy cat scratch disease rather than cancer.

Tuesday came around and I was sent off for my biopsy. I still heard the word "infection" often enough that there was a TINY part of me holding out hope. We waited and waited and waited, until finally Friday arrived and we could follow up with the breast surgeon to remove the drainage tube from my armpit (again, so romantic) and even the anti-social surgeon that hated eye contact told me I looked terrible and would likely be admitted to the hospital later that day. Thankfully, I had an appointment with the director of hematology/oncology at the hospital immediately following that appointment, and she just straight up said it as bluntly as she could, "You have cancer in your body."

If Only This Had Started With A Cat Scratch

I wish I could say I was shocked, but I wasn't. I didn't even cry. All I could think of was, man, my Mom has to sit next to me and hear that her daughter has cancer at age 25. The past week was definitely an emotional roller coaster, but that moment in itself was almost surreal. The doctor couldn't tell us more from there, not that I could have comprehended much more at that point anyhow. She did say that I have cancer in my bones, lungs and lymph nodes, but was unsure what TYPE of cancer I have as they don't know where it originated yet.

To be on the safe side, as cancer often travels from the breast tissue to the lymph nodes, my doctor sent me over to women's health for a mammogram (anyone out there had one of these before? It hurts, my breasts were so twisted and contorted I was almost sure that I would walk out of there with permanent pancakes). For some good news, my breasts are healthy! No sign of breast cancer hanging out in there.

John, my Mom and I packed up and headed to South Dakota to figure out what all of this means and visit with some highly esteemed oncologists/hematologists at Avera in Sioux Falls. Tomorrow will hopefully lead to more answers, and possible a bone biopsy. Worst part, nothing to eat or drink after midnight. It might not seem like a big deal to most people, but for someone who is a mouth breather on these crazy medications I'm taking, it becomes its own battle to not chug a gallon of water every night.

More info to come.

♡Angie

Center's Perspective

On Friday, March 3, Angie called me to say she had gone to the doctor the day before to get the lump under her armpit checked out. This was familiar territory, as she had a different lump removed from her armpit several years earlier when she was in college. She had a breast surgeon do it and they sent it in to be checked. No cancer. Life resumed.

This time, though, Angie also had a dry, nagging cough, was incredibly tired, and her arm constantly hurt. Angie's doctor assumed it was an enlarged lymph node. She did some blood work, took a chest x-ray, and set her up with a referral to a breast surgeon. Angie's primary care doctor told her she would be out of town for a couple weeks and her replacement would follow up with her as to the results from the blood work and x-ray.

Angie called the doctor's office the next day, Friday, to get results and was told her white count was high and she had nodules on her lungs. She was told it could be inflammation, infection, a non-cancerous tumor, or cancerous tumor. She was scheduled to get a CT scan on Monday and the swollen lymph node removed on Tuesday.

Russ and I decided to go to Kansas City on Sunday and stay through Tuesday's biopsy or longer if needed. We got to Kansas City on Sunday afternoon and were very shocked at what we saw. It had only been a few weeks since we had last seen Angie. She had lost so much weight since then and now walked like a beautiful little, old lady, hunched over in pain. Her dry cough was constant. She needed help getting up off the couch or out of bed because of the pain. Reality struck us hard on the face. Something is going on here and it's not good.

As the day went on and into the evening, we were unable to stay on top of the pain with simply Tylenol as our only option and decided she needed to go to the emergency room. It took us 45 minutes to get to the ER as Angie would not allow us to go to the closest one since it wasn't in the best part of town, especially at night.

When we got to the emergency room, we got a wheelchair as walking was not an option between her pain and shortness of breath. Whenever she got worked up, the shortness of breath got considerably worse, so we did everything we could to keep her calm. After we got registered and saw the doctor, he gave her some morphine and the pain eased up tremendously. Then he wanted to do an EKG to look for blood clots in the lungs and since she was scheduled for a CT scan the next day, they also did that to see what was going on.

The doctor came back and told us that she also had spots on her spine and pelvis which was causing the pain and the ones on her lungs were causing the shortness of breath. He wrote her a prescription for pain medication and sent us home.

On the way out of the ER, one of the nurses stopped Russ and gave him a hug. She was crying and told him, "Good luck." No one had told us she had cancer yet. We left to fill the prescription, not an easy task in the middle of a Sunday night. We went back to John and Angie's house, tucked her into bed, and I laid by her so when she woke up I could help her, as she was unable to get out of bed by herself.

Monday we stayed at the house as we already had the CT scan done. Angie tried calling the doctor and didn't get any answers as to what was going on except what was in her online medical chart. The chart screamed cancer when you looked up all the medical terms and connected the dots, but nobody had verbally confirmed this.

I prayed and prayed. In the past, I had always ended my prayers, "Thy will be done," because I always knew God could see the whole picture beginning to end while we can only see what is in front of us. But during this time, I prayed but I couldn't say "Thy will be done," because although I know God's will is best, His will may not be the same as my will. This brought me great anxiety, not ending with "Thy will be done."

Day after day, while waiting for test results and calls back from the doctor, we tried everything we could get our hands on to manage the pain. Patches, Tylenol, ibuprofen, oils, creams, cold and hot packs, baths, etc., nothing helped for very long. Her cough was constant. Nothing soothed it and if she got even a little wound up she had a very difficult time breathing so we were very careful not to upset her. We would make anything she thought sounded good to eat, only to have her eat just two bites. It is so incredibly hard to be a parent when you can't fix it. Russ kept saying, "I'm sorry, I'm sorry." I'd ask, "What for? You didn't do anything to cause this." He replied, "Because I'm the one who fixes their problems and I can't fix this."

Night after night, I slept with Angie and we held hands just so we knew the other was close by. If I didn't sleep with her, I slept with the phone by my ear and she would call or text several times a night for me to bring her medicine or just wanted to talk, and then apologize because she was keeping me awake; as if I could sleep. But that was Angie, always worrying about everyone else first.

Back and forth all week, we called and texted Jessy and Cassy with updates. Jessy was mad and scared as hell. She wanted us to basically throw Angie over our shoulder and drag her to ED screaming and kicking, as if she had enough energy to do that. Cassy was calmer and more unbelieving. She was hopeful and patient, a "just keep calling the doctor and wait and don't borrow trouble" attitude.

I was scared and wanted answers, but I didn't believe calling the doctor continuously was going to help much as she had never seen the same doctor twice. I did believe she needed to see someone right now, but I had to keep reminding myself that Angie is an adult, she has a decision in this. Plus, she needed a little time to process.

Angie never cried about the possibility of cancer that week. I think we all knew that it would be a great change but never imagined the extent of it. We just had a "this sucks, but we'll get through it" attitude. Angie was tough and young and healthy before this happened. The constant pull between Jessy's go-go-go right now, Cassy's wait, they'll call you stance, and our inability to help Angie and seeing our healthy daughter become so weak, so fast, seemed to be tearing us apart. I was scared for Angie and for our family. This was the only time I truly wondered what this was going to do to our extremely close-knit family.

One night while we were down in Kansas City, two of Angie's best friends since elementary school came over and we reminisced and cried. They had been through so much together and they both knew this was just the beginning of a whole new chapter. Angie also received a sunshine package in the mail one day from another close friend, filled with lots of Angie's favorites–everything in yellow. It made her smile to open that bright box filled with homemade goodies and jokes on scraps of paper. It was good to see her friends supporting her already.

You can truly tell how much a man loves your daughter by how he treats her when she is sick. John was so good to her, getting her anything she asked for and anything he thought she might like. But he also gave her enough space as not to suffocate her. I tried my best when John was home to give them all the time they needed as he did for me, too.

Angie was equally strong and weak at the same time. She was unable to get her medicine, get out of bed, or shower by herself but never complained about the circumstances, only the pain.

Tuesday, the day of surgery, Russ, John, Angie, and I were there when the doctor talked to her about before and after the biopsy. He never looked at any of us while we were there. He just plainly told us what he was going to do and then quickly left the room. The plan was to remove four or five lymph nodes. After the procedure was over, he again met with us, still never looking at us. He explained when he got in there that the lymph nodes were all stuck together in clumps, so he removed three clumps of lymph nodes instead of the 4 or 5 individual lymph nodes as planned. He again quickly left the room as if he couldn't wait to get out of there.

Friday came and Angie and I went back to the surgeon who removed the lymph nodes for a follow-up. This time, he looked directly at us and took his time explaining how he had to take the extra lymph nodes. He told Angie, "I see you have an oncology appointment after this. After seeing you on Tuesday and again today, don't be surprised if they put you into the hospital immediately. You look so much worse today." He said goodbye and wished us best of luck in the future.

Before driving to the oncology appointment, Angie and I sat in the car and commented on his remark about getting admitted today and the real possibility of it being cancer. Angie and I discussed where she wanted to receive treatment at and she decided she wanted to come back home, to South Dakota and at least figure it all out. Then once there was a plan in place, she would come back to KC.

Angie asked me, "Mom, is this the hardest thing you have ever went through?" Not yet knowing her full prognosis and believing we would cure it and be stronger for it, I said, "One of the hardest things, yes. This is different, though, because I have to rely on other people to fix it, I cannot fix it."

My mind flashed back to the hardest point in my life, my teenage years when I didn't think that I had enough to offer the world and, because of that, resulted in foster care at age 15. I really was one of the lucky ones because I had wonderful foster parents that kept me in their life forever and always treated me like their own. I was also blessed by both of my parents remarrying and bringing in a bonus Mom and bonus Dad into my life, two more people that really cared about me. All those challenges in the past gave me experience in resilience to rely on as we headed into a new trial.

I drove us to oncology, and if going there wasn't stressful enough,

Angie had to suffer through my driving in a large city. I learned I detest roundabouts.

We got to the oncology department and met the doctor, a very nice woman. Had Angie not decided to seek treatment in Sioux Falls, this woman would've been a good choice for her. I thought this was comforting when thinking of long term treatment options.

The oncologist came straight out with the diagnosis, "Angie, you have cancer in your lungs, lymph nodes, and bones." It was good to finally have some answers. Neither of us cried, we just got teary-eyed. I kept thinking, *This sucks! But we will get through it and it will make us stronger.* The doctor also told us she did not know where the cancer originated and even went back to the lab while we were there to see if they had any more answers yet. A mammogram was requested to be done that day as it is very common to have breast cancer if it is in the lymph nodes.

Then she told Angie she needed to decide where she wanted to get treatment at. Angie told her, "I want to go back to SD because I will have more help, but I don't think I can handle the trip." The doctor replied, "Don't worry about that, I will give you enough pain medication to get you home. Do you have someone to see there?"

While the doctor ran back to the lab, we called a family friend who works in oncology at the hospital in Sioux Falls and got an appointment for 7:00 a.m. Monday morning. The doctor came back without any new answers as to where the cancer started, only that it was Stage 4 and told Angie if she ever needed help when she was in KC, she only had to call her.

When we got back to the car, Angie called John and I called Russ—not an easy thing for either of us. Hearing my baby girl has cancer was the hardest things I have ever had to do, but a close second was telling Russ and the girls. We have been married 34 years and I had only seen him cry once, when his Dad died the previous summer. To hear him cry on the phone broke my heart. I honestly don't remember the girls' exact reaction, not because it wasn't important, but because God knew I could only handle so much at one time. So much to process but it all had to wait as you cannot cry, pray, and drive all at the same time. Angie wanted to go to see her bosses and friends at work and tell them personally what was going on. So, we stopped there on the way back to her house. I don't think they were honestly surprised. However, they were some of the sweetest, most caring people filled with concern for Angie.

We decided to come back to SD on Sunday, as to give us Saturday to pack and let Angie rest because we knew it was going to be a long trip, and not because John was a slow driver.

Jerry's Perspective

On that Friday, I remember sitting at my kitchen table with my Mom during my lunch break. Ang had already been on the phone with Mom earlier that day. Mom placed the call on speaker phone and told Ang to start over and explain it all to me.

I could hear it in her voice right away. She sounded like hell, exhausted and with a dry, persistent cough every few words. But more than that, I could hear the fear in her voice. She explained to me how she had been feeling over the last few weeks. She told me about how unbearable the pain had become and how she had taken the last couple days off work. She told me what the x-ray said about possible metastatic disease and of all the things her doctor said it could be: TB, infection, non-cancerous tumor, cat scratch disease, and cancer. I immediately felt without a doubt in my mind that it was cancer, but I kept that comment to myself.

We went over the options. I don't have anything close to a medical degree, but at this point we had enough family history in and out of hospitals and with a variety of illnesses we could pretty quickly cross many of these possible diagnoses off the list. It was unlikely she contracted TB, she knew no one with it. Cat–scratch disease was not even a real option. Angie despised cats, so it was unlikely she was close enough to any to contract that. Infection–maybe but unlikely. With the severity of the symptoms she was having, one would expect the white count to be through the roof and it was only slightly elevated.

We knew our family tree was full of cancer diagnosis, leukemia, colon cancer, brain cancer, pancreatic cancer, kidney cancer...the list goes on. But all the family members that faced cancer did so a little later in life. Only one was diagnosed under age 30. We cautiously held out hope that it was still something else.

Mom and Dad decided to go to Kansas City on Sunday, so they would be there in time for Angie's appointments and testing on Monday. I remember getting a phone call Sunday night. Ang was worse than they expected when they got there and getting worse as the evening went. She couldn't get out of a chair without help, she was so weak. She could hardly utter a word without erupting into a coughing fit, she was short of breath and hurt so much that she could only curl up in pain.

Mom and Dad communicated this to me on the phone. I encouraged them to go to the ER. "If she is that bad, why are you waiting until morning?" Images of the night before my son, Conrad, was admitted into the hospital for RSV flashed through my brain. His hot little body in the middle of my bed trying to sleep that night, his breathing getting so sketchy that we questioned taking him to the ER but decided to wait until morning. Taking him into his appointment that morning his oxygen barely dipping down. Seeing him worsen throughout the day until there was no choice but to place him on a ventilator that evening. He wasn't just sick, he was fighting for every breath, fighting for his life. He was not quite four months old. I know how lucky we were that Conrad did not take a turn for the worst at home, that he did so in the care of hospital staff who were prepared to handle the situation. I was suddenly terrified that Ang would take a turn for the worst before they even knew what was wrong with her.

She got pain meds in the ER, which helped. They ruled out anything that would be considered an emergency and sent her home. Later, I'd find out that Ang knew with utmost certainty she had cancer after that visit. She said she could see it in the eyes of the doctor as he told her about her "scary spots," never officially diagnosing her with cancer as that wasn't his place. She knew from the way the nurse gave her and Dad a teary-eyed hug as she left; a nurse she had met just a couple hours before. Unspoken, she was diagnosed with cancer in that ER.

Monday came and, with the pain meds she was sent home with, she was able to cope until her biopsy on Tuesday. I still talked to Mom, Dad, and Ang multiple times a day. Without being told, we all were putting together the pieces of the puzzle; the chest x-ray with the radiologist report that showed on her online chart and stated innumerable ill-defined nodules in her lungs, the CT scan that showed the spots on her spine and pelvis, the enlarged lymph nodes. If this was cancer, we knew that qualified it as stage 4; but it remained unspoken, even among us. No one wanted it to be true. Angie did not want anyone outside our immediate family to know what was occurring. She was reluctant to let Grandmama know, she didn't want her to be worried, but with Dad and Mom suddenly out of town, she had to be let in on what was happening. Mom and Dad asked me to talk to her. The conversation was hard. Grandmama is one of the toughest women I know. She raised us as much as our own parents. As I explained the pain Ang was in, the possibilities for diagnosis, and the test results and appointments they were awaiting, I could see Grandmama trying her best to hold it all in. Trying to once again be strong. It wasn't the first time.

When my grandma was in high school, she lost her father to Hodgkin's lymphoma. In her twenties, she lost her sister to leukemia at the young age of 39. She prayed for her mother, as she fought and defeated cervical cancer. Years later, she again lifted her Mom up in prayer during her final days as pancreatic cancer took her life. She watched her husband battle and defeat colon cancer. She stood by her son, Mark, while he was diagnosed with kidney cancer, cared for him during his treatment, celebrated when he beat it and cautiously watched him fight again when he was diagnosed with a sarcoma a few years later. She cried with her youngest son, Doug, as he went through a hard patch in his life, only to be made harder with a diagnosis of hairy cell leukemia and cried again tears of joy when, by a miracle, he went into remission. No this wasn't the first time that my Grandmama had to be strong. She had more experience in this uncertainty than any of us.

Angie's pain meds only did their trick for a while. Tuesday came, and they did the biopsy as scheduled and sent her home to wait for results. She was continuing to fail. Each day her pain getting worse, her breathing getting harder, her cough just as nagging. Dad came back from Kansas City alone, as he had to get back to work. Mom stayed with Ang, and via phone I continued to beg them to push her doctors harder. To call them more frequently, to make sure they were aware of how much pain she was in, how hard her breathing was, to go to a different ER if it is as bad as they were saying. Every day seemed like a week when I was so many miles away and only getting bits and pieces.

Conversations quietly began among our family, cautiously speaking of cancer and where she would seek treatment if it was. We all encouraged her to come to Sioux Falls, where we knew doctors and hospital staff. All of our family was here and she would have more support. I begged for Mom to just bring her home now, we would sort it out in Sioux Falls. Ang wanted to wait until she received word from her doctor on her biopsy, continually reminding me, "It could still be an infection."

Sure, Mom and Ang were starting to more openly discuss the likely diagnosis, but they were also in a phase of denial. They knew what was happening but didn't want it to be true. Every phone call to check in, I could hear them getting more and more defensive, trying to justify the possibility of infection, burying themselves in Ang's house, hoping to ignore it and it would go away.

Throughout all of this I tried to keep my husband, Kyle, up to speed as to what was going on. He brushed it off. *Ang is fine, she is overreacting. Everyone is overreacting. Quit being Dr. Google. You are not a doctor.* Each time I brought it up the concern would quickly pass his face and he would become easily annoyed at the conversation. He had no interest in being my sounding board. He was certain everything was being blown out of proportion.

Cassy was somewhere in between Kyle and I. She was getting updates constantly. She was still on Angie's side, patting her back long distance every time she said, "It could still be an infection." She was in denial, too. I had to choose my words carefully around her to keep from upsetting her.

On Wednesday, Mom called while I was visiting Grandmama again. Ang was worse. She was in so much pain. Mom was upset. As Ang and Mom talked through what was happening and how the pain meds were no longer doing enough, I became irate. No one was listening to me. All of us knew this was cancer, but Mom and Ang were doing their best to isolate themselves from the real world and the doctors were not giving it the urgency it needed. Why weren't they doing more? And there standing in my grandma's dining room on the phone, I again pushed for them to go back to the ER, for them to contact her doctor again, for them to go to a different hospital, for them to "JUST GET IN THE #@(%!#% CAR AND DRIVE HER HOME." I just went off, screaming and swearing through the tears. So afraid I was going to lose my sister before anyone even figured out what she had.

I have never used such language to my Mom. Or in front of my grandma. Or within the walls of Grandma's home, our second home and sanctuary throughout our childhood.

On Friday, March 10, Angie had her first appointment with the oncology doctor in Kansas City to review all of the tests that occurred over the last week, the chest x-ray, the bloodwork, the CT scan. Biopsy results were not yet in. She was officially diagnosed with cancer at that appointment. Angie immediately made the decision to go to Sioux Falls for treatment. My Dad was already pulling strings to get her in to the first appointment available with the oncology group that worked a miracle on his brother, Doug. It was by the pure grace of God that Doug ended up in the hands of the right doctor who was able to find the right clinical trial that saved his life. Our family was now looking to this same doctor again, praying he had another miracle.

Ang, John, and Mom made it home to the farm, hoping to rest before her 7:00 a.m. appointment on Monday in Sioux Falls. On Sunday, my family and Cassy's went over to our parents for dinner and to see Ang for the first time since all this began. She looked like hell that day. Weak, pale, unable to get out of furniture on her own, constantly coughing a dry, hacking cough that took her breath away. She was using the pain meds the oncologist gave her before sending her off to Sioux Falls, but they just took the edge off.

She was visibly sick, and I was so fearful of what the doctors would discover the following day. I knew enough people who had been diagnosed with cancer and very rarely were they visibly sick. Most diagnoses came out of the blue where the patient was maybe feeling a little off or found a lump with no symptoms. Most cancer diagnosis were not like this.

Cassy's Perspective

Angie was my person. The relationship we had was unique and different to everyone else's in my life. As cliché as it may sound, we weren't just sisters, she was my best friend. We could go days without speaking but always just picked up where we left off. Never upset with the other for not answering the phone or texting the other first. We had inside jokes, shared one another's deep, dark secrets, and could make each other laugh so hard that no noise was being made, just our shoulders shaking and eyes watering while trying to catch our breaths. My Mom knew if she was sensing something wasn't right with Angie but couldn't get enough information out of her that she'd have to sick me on her like some kind of drug dog searching for clues.

One Thursday evening Mom said to me, "You know Cas, Ang hasn't been feeling very good lately. Maybe you should give her a call, see how she's doing?"

So that evening I found a few minutes between an appointment and running home to be with my kids and I gave her a ring. I remember her sounding tired and thinking, "What does she have going on to be so tired from? I'm the one with two boys under the age of three, she must really not be feeling well."

She gave me a rundown of her symptoms but then the conversation turned more into her upcoming trip to Mexico and how were the kids and I hung up hoping she'd be feeling better by the end of the weekend.

Never in my wildest dreams did I think a week later we would facing the biggest nightmare of our family's lives. As the days went on that week things went from bad to worse at 100 miles an hour. Angie went from having significant pain to being in complete agony.

I am the peacemaker in the family, I don't do confrontation, and I hate drama. My parents were petrified, Jessy was irate, and I was becoming the monkey in the middle. I'd talk to Jessy or Dad and I'd want to jump in the car and haul her home. Then I would speak with Mom and Ang they would sugar coat things so thick I figured she must be OK. Back and forth like a tennis ball I'd go from one extreme to the next. Fact of the matter was we were all scared. Dad and Jessy showed it in frustration. Frustration that she still didn't have a diagnosis. Mom and Ang were scared that the diagnosis would come and there'd be no going back. Every time I heard that "C" word mentioned, denial took over. I'd shut down. This can't be happening. It's not real.

Guess what? It was real. When we saw Angie that Sunday it sunk in fast and hard. How much weight she had lost, her glasses and clothes swallowing her. How frail she looked. How exhausted. How she could barely speak without coughing. My sister has cancer. MY SISTER has CANCER. Yet she's acting like she hadn't even noticed, chit chatting with my boys in the car. Helping my husband secure airline tickets for a work trip. Acting normal. For me, she was avoiding the very, very large elephant in the room. She knew that seeing her that way was killing me. I don't do well with confrontation and this demon was staring me right in the eyes.

John's Perspective

A harmless Sunday hangout session at my friend's house. That's how it all started for me, that's where I first met Angie. I was back in Brookings visiting friends and family. I was living in Denver at the time, and during that particular "Sunday hangout," I remember to this day thinking, Angie is pretty good looking! We were all recovering from each of our Saturday night prior, so it was a (makeup-free) sweatpant and movie kind of day! I only say that because, to me, that's who Angie was in my eyes throughout. She was a beautiful person to the core, not needing to cover-up any flaws.

Fast forward about a year from that memory. I had finally found a company I felt would provide me a long-term career path months earlier. I was freshly relocated to the Midwest (Kansas City) for my job, not far from where I was raised (South Dakota). When I relocated, it was close to the holidays, so naturally I traveled back to Brookings where I still had a brother and friends. Wouldn't you know it, that subtle thought of Angie crept back into my head, and all of a sudden the idea of dating her became a thought! In all actuality, it became more than a thought, because a few months later we were in fact dating! It was early in the relationship but I immediately saw the qualities she possessed. She was smart, witty, kind, and caring to name a few. All of those features are what people look for in a partner, but what I loved the most is the way she could make me smile. She had a humor that I appreciated and thought was unique in itself.

Long distance relationships can be tough, and ours proved no different. We struggled the first year, through times that seemed too difficult or too much work to make worthwhile. When she was accepted at Missouri State University in Springfield, Missouri, things got better. That is when we really relied on one another. We would split trips between KC and Springfield until we moved in together at an apartment in KC. At that point, our relationship really "blossomed!"

"How loving was she?" I swear Kona smiles because every day Angie came home from work, she would get so excited with pets and a high-pitched praise and love that he'd go nuts! To this day, people comment about how he shows his upper teeth (gums and all!), to the point that it even scares kids and adults until they realize it's not a growl just a cheesy smile!

"How kind was she?" Find any co-worker or child who visited her clinic. I know she made every one of them feel loved, as she patiently would wait at times at the clinic sometimes more than an hour until the last patient and child would get a ride back home.

"How caring was she?" Ask any new mother (friend, family, or stranger) who asked Angie for advice about child nutrition.

"How patient was she?" Find out more about me, then realize she was willing to spend the rest of her life with this at times impatient person!

It's hard not to play Monday morning quarterback and think of all the signs you missed, or to think of the "what ifs" by doing something different throughout her sickness. Aside from just missing having her around, it's probably the hardest part to grasp and be at ease with, at least for myself. Tiredness, fatigue, lack of appetite, weight loss, and swollen lymph nodes, just some potential signs, to name a few. Angie was an early riser in the mornings, often leaving before or as the sun was rising to get ahead of traffic to ease any anxieties. She'd work through the day and be home usually around 6PM. It wasn't far-fetched if soon after dinner she fell asleep for a nap or just go to bed early in the night. So tiredness and fatigue were hard to measure. She was all about portion control, so the lack of appetite also was hard to find a drastic change.

The lymph node was the most obvious but I felt when she noticed it, and when we discussed it, she mentioned the previous breast tissue she had removed so I wasn't overly worried initially. It was short–lived and as with much of her sickness, it would be a fast-paced cramming session of learning and addressing. After a few weeks, it was noticeable that she didn't have energy and would just go straight to bed when she came home. Weight loss was now being mentioned by Angie. Again only a few weeks, so maybe this was just a bug she had caught, too, now? She finally agreed that maybe she needed to go to the doctor, get the swollen area in her arm looked at, and just figure out what if anything is happening to her. Angie was always very intuitive, she could sense when things weren't right, whether that was with me, our relationship, or other various things. It was always odd to me how she would mention cancer throughout our relationship, her family history, what if she ever got it? I can't help but think that there was a part of her that possibly knew what was happening, but didn't want to face that. I'll never know, but I'll always speculate.

The post doctor visit is where I started to get a little heightened in my senses. Still optimistic but thoughts began to creep in my head when she said they were going to have a surgery to remove the inflamed tissue and test it to ensure it wasn't cancerous. Anytime you hear the C-word used, it's hard not to think about a worst case scenario type of situation. Five months prior, I had just lost a close friend to lung cancer, lightning couldn't strike twice was my general thinking.

All of a sudden, the process couldn't be fast enough. The surgery needing to be performed couldn't be for days later in the week. Results would take "X amount of days," which was not soon enough. I just remember feeling trapped, in a sense. We had started a process but couldn't pick up and leave to repeat it somewhere else, we would be losing all of that time we put in and be at the same merciful process with another hospital. Finally, we were at a point where we could go to Sioux Falls and be closer to our home state to get a game plan together. The drive back has been made what feels like 100 times by now with visits home and holidays had in South Dakota. This drive was very different and seemed much longer. Angie was now in great pain, to the point where managing it with over the counter drugs was not working. I remember talking with Russ before we left and we both had a sense that whatever was coming up was going to be anything but an easy process. We drove to South Dakota on a Sunday and straight to the hospital in Sioux Falls, Monday.

CHAPTER 2

Alternative Truths

CARINGBRIDGE POST
by Angela Hazel, March 13, 2017

If this message makes any sense at all, I will be very surprised! Oxygen taped to my finger, IVs all tangled up in the bedsheets, and the pain killers doing their job likely leads to a poorly spelled and grammatically incorrect next 500 characters. Bear with me.

Today was a blur. We arrived at Avera around 7 a.m. to meet with the doctor and come up with game plan. The biggest challenge we've faced today is that we STILL do not have a biopsy back from the lymph node they excised last Tuesday in KC. Without knowing what type of cancer I have exactly, it's hard (almost impossible) to move forward with a treatment plan. So what did we do in the meantime? Every other test imaginable. It started off with bloodwork, a spinal tap and a bone marrow biopsy. While the doctor was working on my back and a needle was shoved up my spine, they did a round of chemo because my dr is very concerned with how quickly my cancer is growing and spreading.

This is where my day begins to get very fuzzy. After the biopsy, I began to have the worst pain imaginable that we couldn't get on top of. I did a chest x-ray to compare the new x-ray to the one done in KC last Friday, and found more gray spots/fluid on my lungs. Since I didn't bounce back after the spinal tap, chest x-ray and bone marrow biopsy as expected, they decided to admit me to Avera and see how things went overnight.

The afternoon was a blur of nurses, doctors and pain medications as we tried to figure out the best way to keep me comfortable. The doctor followed up with an echocardiogram and while we haven't gotten the official results yet, the tech felt that I have a healthy heart based on his preliminary assessment, no apparent fluid on my heart. Whoop!

I did have problems with keeping my oxygen levels normal during the day and have been on continuous oxygen since arrival at the Prairie Center this morning. This is likely due to the gray spots on my lungs that are causing me to be short of breath. I've been experiencing night sweats and random fevers, with my fever peaking over 100 degrees today, but the medication brought this back down and I was explained to me that the fever is normal, it's just by body still trying to fight off whatever it is that is making me so ill.

I believe tomorrow we are scheduled for a port placement, but like I said, I've been in and out of consciousness all afternoon, so I'll have to have John and my Mom fact-check me so I'm not spreading "alternative truths". ;)

This outpour of love and support from everyone has been indescribable. I thank you all so much for your constant words of love, prayer, countless text messages and the beautiful flowers, cards, and chocolates. I feel so lucky to have such amazing people in my life that care for me!

♡Angie

Carter's Perspective

Monday morning came early, we met with the hematologist, an incredibly nice doctor who explained all the tests they would do and why. He told us Angie could go home after the testing was completed that day and come back the next day for an MRI, as that is the only way insurance would pay for it.

That day, Angie met a beautiful woman who would have a significant impact on her life, a Prairie Center Chaplin. They connected immediately. God had truly sent this chaplain to help Angie through everything. Angie had many pastors coming to visit her throughout her battle and she liked them all because they all contributed something to help her or someone in our family along the way, but this one seemed to touch her soul. She was Angie's angel on earth.

As the day went on, it didn't take long for plans to change. While they were doing the bone marrow testing, Angie was given a dose of chemo. Each hour she continued to get sicker and sicker, at times unable to communicate with us. Her doctor decided she would be hospitalized. As she got worse throughout the day, we repeatedly kept hearing, "we don't have much time."

Angie was admitted into the hospital and we met many more significant people that day. They all were so much more than just their job title, all were people who truly cared. I spent the night with Angie. It brought both of us tremendous comfort knowing all we had to do was open our eyes and know we were not alone.

Jerry's Perspective

Angie used one of her brief moments of strength to update her CaringBridge that Monday. She was wore out from all the testing. We were all thankful for the thoroughness of the oncology team. It was immediately clear to our family that she was in the right place for her treatment by the degree of urgency and concern the doctors showed to her from the first moment she entered their doors. Plus, she was only 45 minutes from my parent's house, a welcome blessing to close family who all lived nearby. Home wasn't far, yet Mom and John stayed right there at the hospital with her day and night.

Her doctor, the same one my uncle had, was amazing. He had a way of explaining things clearly, expressing the urgency and the seriousness of the situation while doing the best he could to console our family and ease our fears.

We took turns sitting in the small room with Ang, being a second or third set of ears to absorb the doctor's updates, and comforting each other in the waiting room or the chapel. We all rallied behind Angie. I browsed Amazon during the downtime, adding t-shirts to my cart with "!*#% CANCER" and "I don't have enough middle fingers for this disease!" blasted across them. We were certain this was just a bump in her road, a chapter in her book. We discussed that the strongest people in life have the biggest challenges, certain God would lead her through this difficulty and it would launch her into her greater purpose as an inspiration to others.

Ang went in and out of consciousness those first few days, finally starting to get a little relief from the immense pain she had been in, through the better pain management that the hospital staff was able to offer her. Those first couple days were a blur for everyone as each hour presented new tests, new information, but no clear diagnosis beyond "cancer." It was clear that all the doctors were digging in, but it was also clear that she was an exception to most patients.

Cassy's Perspective

Apparently, I'm a lot more of a visual person than I ever realized. It took physically seeing Angie for me to really let her diagnosis sink in. Actually, sinking in is probably an over statement. More like seeing Angie allowed me to barely begin to absorb the fact that she was sick. I knew as each test came and went our lives were forever changed. Each test that revealed more problems than answers, meant that I'd never again have a "normal" day. Pre-cancer diagnosis and post-cancer diagnosis was like black and white. And why the hell couldn't these doctors figure out what kind it was or where it originated? Was not being able to diagnose someone even a thing these days?

I quietly observed my family from the corner of the hospital room. Dad like a chicken with his head chopped off, trying to complete tasks that no father should be needing to worry about for his 25-year-old daughter. How does a man with a family full of women to take care of deal with that many hormones swarming at once? Mom, trying to be two steps ahead at all moments, keeping Angie as comfortable as possible and soaking in every minute with her. You could look into her eyes and see a movie reel of Angie's childhood memories playing on repeat. Jes, balls to the wall, hating cancer so much that I thought she'd pummel the next doctor or nurse who came in that didn't have a cure-all solution written on their prescription pad. She would go from sobbing to hatred back and forth. More passion in her pinkie finger than most had in their entire bodies. We were coping so completely opposite. And then there was John, Angie's knight in shining armor. He was like an angel you see in movies with a glowing halo above his head in her eyes. The one who could push her fears away. We all had our roles. Mom kept saying, "We can't all fall apart on the same day," so I kept on holding it together.

Cinters Perspective

Tuesday morning came and seemed to be more of a turning point. The doctors were no longer focusing on what type of cancer she was facing as the priority, instead they switched gears to "what can we do to slow this down." It was a whirlwind. The doctors decided to go with IMAP chemo, the strongest, broadest chemo they could find as they still had no idea where the cancer started. They planned to begin in the next morning. They explained to Angie that they would also give her a drug to stop her cycle, to attempt to protect her ovaries and eggs so that someday she maybe could have babies. It was discussed that ideally, they would harvest and save her eggs, but once again they said there was not enough time. It seemed like every time we turned around the doctors were telling us there was not enough time.

Also, on Tuesday the Palliative Care team came to visit Angie and us for the first time. Up to this point, I didn't even know this type of care team existed. They wanted to ask end of life questions.

What the hell?! I thought. *She was just admitted yesterday, and you want to bury her already? No, you need to leave. None of us can deal with this now.* As horrible as it sounds, I disliked those people before I even knew their names.

It seemed all of us were settling into our new jobs. Russ handling finances, me and Jessy, the medical questions, and John and Cassy keeping the calm.

CHAPTER 3

You All Are Babies…

CARINGBRIDGE POST
by Jessy Paulson, March 15, 2017

This journal entry is coming from me, John, Anita, and Russ with a little assistance from Ang. I am certain we are nowhere near as good of writers as she is so bear with us!

Today, they are starting Angie on chemo. They have made a diagnosis of Stage 4 Cancer of Unknown Primary. They suspect it is a very aggressive sarcoma and are beginning chemo treatments for that. This morning they began a 48-hour chemo treatment that is followed by 4 weeks rest.

Angie is very in and out due to the massive amount of pain meds going through her system to make her comfortable, the chemo treatments and her general discomfort as the cancer progresses. She is fighting like hell and maintaining her sense of humor throughout it all. In fact, within the last hour we were looking for more tissues and she said, "I just had a box here, you all must be babies."

Right now, we are limiting visitors, also because she is in the oncology unit she cannot have flowers and such. All we need is prayers and your continued love and support sent this way while she fights.
Pray hard.

Carter's Perspective

Wednesday morning, Angie's doctors were in bright and early. They discussed the plan for the day in starting Angie on IMAP chemo and going forward with Angie, John and me. I had a hard time concentrating, as I had a question I couldn't ask in front of Angie. I followed the doctor out to the hallway when they left, even though this was something Angie absolutely hated and told us so. (Russ did it quite often until we all caught hell from her.) But this morning, it could not be helped, I had to know.

I stopped the doctor and said, "I need to know in black and white. You guys keep saying we don't have much time. What exactly does that mean? If Angie would choose not to do chemo, even though she is going to do it, if she chose not to, how long would she have? And if she does do chemo, what are we looking at?" John and myself were standing in the hallway speaking with the doctors. I glanced up and saw my foster sister was walking down the other end of the hallway, on her way for her daily visit.

The doctor said, "Without chemo, she would have about two weeks. With chemo, *and it has to make a significant difference,* we are looking at six months at the most." In that instant, my world tilted and became blurry. I went to the chapel on that floor by myself and broke down completely.

I had cried before but only a little, before pulling myself back together for Angie. This time it felt as if my heart was being ripped from my chest. It hurt so bad. The line had been drawn between honoring the wishes she had as much as we could and living life to the fullest as her body would allow while keeping the hope alive because God can provide miracles.

Once I pulled myself together again, I went to go back to sit with Angie. As I walked by the waiting room, I saw John in there crying. John had been so strong through all of this always looking for a way to make Angie smile or laugh, but this reality was incredibly hard to process. John, like most men I know, is very private about his feelings and seeing him sit there alone, crying, broke my heart. I decided to call Russ at work and told him I knew it was a crappy way for him to find out, but he needed to know right away so he could make plans to be gone at work. Fortunately, his workplace was there to help him with whatever he needed to make this easier for him.

Jerry's Perspective

Within a day or so in Sioux Falls, they confirmed everything the Kansas City testing suggested. Angie had cancer in her lymph nodes, on her pelvis, on her spine, and in her lungs. It was everywhere. Each hour was excruciating, the doctor offering hope that when the biopsy results from Kansas City came back he would know what type of cancer she had and therefore a direction to go to treat the cancer.

They did discover, fairly quickly, that the cancer was not a leukemia or a lymphoma. With this news, came a change in doctors. The doctor our family had called upon to save Ang could now not treat her as he was a hematologist, not an oncologist. He promised he placed her in the best hands and continued to stay updated on her case but this created another unknown for our family. We trusted him, he was our miracle worker, he saved Doug's life. This new doctor was highly accredited and acclaimed by the staff at the hospital, but at first impression, he wasn't as personable. It was upsetting she had to change doctors, we had finally felt that we found the right place for Angie's treatment and now were questioning it again. But all we could do is trust that the man in front of us was the best person for the job, that God placed the right people in her life at that moment.

Unknown to us as to why the biopsy results were taking so long, we eventually found out that the Kansas City pathology did every stain possible and sent a piece of it on to San Diego for further evaluation as there was no clear indication of where the cancer originated. I will never forget that conversation. Angie's new oncologist, who had been keeping up to date with her case since she arrived and working closely with the hematologist, sat in Angie's hospital room that afternoon with our family, Angie and John, Mom and Dad and Cassy and me. Her room was barely bigger than the walk-in closet she had at her home in Kansas City. He explained to us the extent of her cancer, how far it had spread, and that there was no clear origin for it but that they suspected it originated as a sarcoma. He diagnosed her with Stage 4 Cancer of Unknown Primary.

He expressed the urgency of getting her started on chemotherapy immediately to try to slow down the progression, to buy more time to figure out what it was and how to treat it. He was moving forward with a chemo regimen the Mayo Clinic uses, the most aggressive, broad spectrum chemotherapy out there. She began a 48-hour chemo treatment that day, along with several supporting medications to protect various organs and to try to keep her as comfortable as possible.

Her doctor explained that there wasn't much time to turn this around, the next few days were vital. She was in very rough shape, as we knew, but he expressed that this chemotherapy was critical in determining how much time she had.

In a conversation with Angie, in which she was going in and out of consciousness from the mass quantity of meds in her system, he told us that these next few days would determine Angie's path. If she responded to the strong chemotherapy, then she would have months. If she did not respond, then she would only have a couple weeks or days if things really took a turn for the worse and she contracted a secondary infection.

Ang caught bits and pieces as she drifted in and out from consciousness.

What did he say?

You All Are Babies...

What do you mean you don't know what it is?

You are giving up on me already?! I can't believe this. I know I have cancer but I can't even fight?

We were trying to absorb the conversation while trying to offer her hope and calm her down. It was impossible.

We were devastated. In all the conversations and thoughts that we had prior to this, we never expected that she would not have a fighting chance. We never expected that she could be within days of the end of her life. Her doctor offered the best hope he could, that if anyone could beat the odds, it would be someone young and in perfect health ordinarily, someone just like Angie. Our conversations then focused on that. *If anyone could beat this, it was Ang.*

This moment in time was a blur for all of us. Angie was drifting in and out all day and night while doctors came into the room trying to have very serious conversations with her and our family. The vast amounts of pain medication and, unbeknown to anyone at this point, a reaction to an anti-anxiety medication that was causing hallucinations for Ang, made it almost impossible for her to have a coherent conversation. It was constantly a battle to absorb what was occurring, and yet keep Ang calm and hopeful. A battle all of us fought but no one more than John, Mom and Dad.

The next day, additional doctors came in, including a palliative care team again, to meet with Angie and our whole family. She was told that due to the aggressiveness of the cancer, the urgency to start treatment, and her current condition, they would be unable to save her eggs. There just wasn't enough time. Angie was heartbroken. Hearing that she would be unable to have children of her own one day was more unbearable than hearing she had Stage 4 cancer. She was devastated that even if she was able to beat this, she would never bear her own children, even by surrogate, and questioned if she even wanted to fight if that was the outcome.

Everything Ang ever wanted, everything a 25-year-old thinks they have time to do, was all crashing in around her. There was not time, life was not going to be as she expected, or as any of us expected.

Difficult conversations regarding end of life care also had to occur. All this did was upset Angie further in her disoriented state, and all of us in our state of shock. They were valid, important questions, asking if Angie would want to be placed on a ventilator if that decision needed to be made at some point, asking who should make medical decisions if she could not make them. Hard questions that no one wanted to think about and just pissed off everyone. It felt like they were already planning her death before she even had a chance to fight.

Cassy's Perspective

We were all babies, Ang was absolutely right. It was hard walking into that hospital room and seeing someone who was so full of life just a couple weeks ago now so close to death. Thinking you had decades of memories to make and realizing you only had days. Trying to hold together a full-time job, being a wife and a mom never left enough time for Ang. I was petrified that this drugged stupor was the state my sister would be in for the rest of her life. To me, this was the scariest time for me in her whole journey. I could handle the diagnosis, I couldn't handle not being able to talk to her. How could I get through a lifetime of not talking to my best friend? I decided from there on out I wasn't going to let any future good moments with her be ruined with ugly crying about how much cancer sucked. There was nothing I could do about it other than pray. So, I was going to treat her like "Angie my sister," not "Angie the cancer patient," like many others seemed to be.

News was spreading like wildfire in our small, sleepy town. After a couple CaringBridge and Facebook posts people began to whisper. "Did you hear about that Hazel girl?" "Yeah, she's got cancer, stage

4." "Poor thing."

Working in the public eye every day it was impossible to escape the sad eyes, the sympathetic pats on my hand, and trying not to break down after having to explain that no the doctors still didn't know what kind it was for the 100th time that day. You see, because living in a small town means you know every Tom, Dick and Harry, they remember that cute, blonde Homecoming queen with the beautiful smile and bubbly personality cheerleading and at the top of the honor roll each year. In that same breath, every Tom, Dick, and Harry was supporting us, rallying behind Angie and lifting her up in prayer. Our pleas to God grew from a few small voices to hundreds and hundreds. The outpouring of love and concern was surreal, humbling, and gave us a sense of hope.

Home was a whole different story, as a mother of an adorable 8-month-old and a very smart, almost 3-year-old I had to be careful of what I could say within ear shot. My oldest, Haizen, knew something was going on with his Aunt Gigi. Gigi was sick, he knew, but I didn't want to scare him. He knew death far too well after watching his great-grandfather pass away only the previous summer. I think I was scared of the hard questions I knew he'd start asking again. Death is complicated enough when the person is elderly, when they are as young as your mama how does that make sense to a young child? So I kept a brave face, never breaking down. I didn't know if I let those tears flow if they'd ever stop.

Becoming a mother was something all three of us girls wanted badly from very early on. When a cancer diagnosis started to become a real possibility for Angie, Jessy and I grew worried that becoming pregnant was something that may not be easy or even possible for Ang. Thoughts of freezing eggs and surrogacy were going through my head. I knew if there were any way to make my sister's dreams possible I would do it. Unfortunately, all within those first couple days of treatment we realized this would not be an option, it was more important to try to save her life than waste any more time. It didn't matter that she had baby names picked out since junior high or that she had taught dozens of new mamas how to nurse their babies all while dreaming of it being her little one someday. It didn't matter she had been "practicing" on her nieces and nephews for the last 11 years and being the best aunt ever, picturing what they'd look like if they were hers. The decision was made, that door was closed. Angie knew it was her only option to begin her aggressive chemo immediately, but it still broke her heart. So many dreams being crushed in that tiny little hospital room.

John's Perspective

In a light-hearted term for this week, I coined it Angie's "Woodstock Week!" Five days of haze, little to no memory or comprehension of her surrounding or the urgency of what was occurring. For her friends and family, I would call it more of "Hell Week." A week where we didn't know if we would make it. Literally, doctors were informing us that this cancer was at stage 4, and there was a very real possibility she wouldn't make it through the next seven days. So in the span of two weeks, you find out you may have cancer, to a point that you may not live through the week because of cancer. Very difficult to process that information for everyone involved.

Angie was essentially lethargic during the week. It felt like the Adam Sandler movie *50 First Dates*, where I would have to share the same difficult news each day to her as if it was the first time she had heard it. Her face was often puzzled, looking at me asking difficult questions about what was happening and if she was going to make it. I had to be honest each time and find answers that would be truthful but leave room for optimism. One of the hardest conversations I've ever had in my life, repeated four days in a row.

CHAPTER 4

Tuna Salad Smelling MRI Machine

CARINGBRIDGE POST
by Angela Hazel, March 17, 2017

Today has been a good day. I've been coming out of my drug induced blackout of the past 3 days and starting to remember more. My last chemo treatment was yesterday so we will wait and see the prognosis over the next couple weeks. Wednesday, they noticed a lot of fluid on my lungs, did an ultrasound and drained both lungs. Today's lung X-ray looked much better and removing the fluid allowed me to breathe much easier.

John planned a surprise for me this morning...I finally got to see my Kona dog after 4 days! He arranged a little meeting outside the hospital and I'm not sure whose smile was bigger, mine or Kona's. Sometimes John knows what the best therapy for me is, even more so than all these doctors. (Side note from something I read on Instagram...Why are veterinarians not called dogcters? Rhetorical) Like I mentioned earlier, the past 3 days I've been in and out and I can't recall much of those days. It's a good thing because the chemo treatment they had me on was pretty intense from the sounds of it. I was talking even crazier than normal, which is saying a lot coming from me. Evidently, I went on a rant about a tuna sandwich smelling MRI machine.... if you know me at all, you know the smell of tuna makes me want to vomit. Luckily, I got out of there without making a mess.

I've been trying to respond to messages here and there but apologize if I missed your text or call. I just want to say thank you for all the love and support from everyone, and I tremendously appreciate the amount of love shown to my family and John/his family over the past few days. This is as much a battle for them as it is for me, maybe more so because I was knocked out for most of it. A special shout-out to John, my parents and sisters for being rock stars and making sure I've always had what I've needed. Sending love.

♡Angie

Center's Perspective

Angie finally went for her MRI that we were hoping to do the first day she arrived in Sioux Falls. Since Angie is a little claustrophobic, medication was given to her to calm down her anxiety level. Whether it was the medication or God making her shut down to process, the next three days she was in and out and hallucinating. She kept bringing up the same conversation repeatedly. "They gave me a shot to protect my ovaries, right? So, I can have babies someday, right? Did I understand that right, Mom?" Over and over, whenever she would wake for a brief period of time. I just kept answering her, "Yes, Angie. They gave you a shot. Don't worry about it right now. Everything will be OK."

After the three days had passed, and Angie was starting to get adjusted to her new normal, she asked if we were given a timeline on how long this would go on. I asked her if she wanted to know what the doctor said about life expectancy.

She replied yes, then no, and then "I'm not sure." I told her if the time ever came that she was certain she wanted to know, to ask again, as I wasn't going to bring it up again until she was ready, if ever, to hear it.

Cassy's birthday came and went with very little acknowledgement. I felt bad, not just about her birthday but about both girls in general. I should be there supporting and helping them through this more....and I couldn't. I simply didn't have the energy. I love them with my whole heart and just prayed they would understand.

Jenny's Perspective

One of the nights that first week, I remember waking up in the early morning hours, sometime around 4:00 a.m. in a state of panic. I don't even know how to describe it except I just felt something was wrong and that I needed to be with Angie. Knowing that she was not alone and if anything was critically wrong, I would get a call or text, even in the middle of the night, I tried to go back to sleep but felt restless and uneasy so instead I left home to head up to the hospital for an early morning visit. I got to the hospital sometime around 5:00 a.m. or so. Ang was sleeping but I found out she had been having some significant pain during the night. I quietly spoke to John to let him know I was there and suddenly her eyes popped open and she asked me what I was doing there. Not wanting to worry her I simply said, "I couldn't sleep so I thought I'd come visit you early today." She looked deep into my eyes and simply said, "God told you to come, God knew I needed you."

Those first few days in the hospital were some of the hardest. We were not only coming to grips with the prognosis Angie was facing, but due to all the medications in her and pain she was in, Angie was not remembering the conversations. Several times, hard discussions had to be repeated, which flared up all emotions again,, raw and more painful each time. The detail Ang received in her recaps depended on who was giving it to her. Our close-knit family started getting angry with each other as we tried to find the balance of providing her hope and giving her the information she deserved to know.

I kept trying to put myself in her place. If I was faced with that devastation, what would I want my family to do for me? I felt very strongly that Angie needed to know what she was up against. She needed to know that this was her one shot and that if she had anyone she wanted to see or anything she wanted to say, it needed to happen. I was on one end of the spectrum while Mom and Cassy were most concerned with keeping her attitude positive and providing hope, so she continued to fight as hard as possible.

After the chemo treatment was through, Angie started to crawl out of her disoriented state and her personality really began to shine once again. The hospital staff was falling in love with her, often nurses would stop in to say hi, even if they were not attending to her that day. It was amazing to see the connections that she had made over her life appear in this unlikely scenario. Old roommates of friends from college, an old classmate of my Dad's, a family friend and neighbor. All these people were placed into Angie's life much earlier on, and now appearing again and providing tremendous care and support to her and our family in our time of need. Very quickly Mom started to refer to these people and events as "God Things." And they were, it was the only clear explanation for perfect timing of exactly what and who we needed.

The day John arranged for Kona to meet Angie outside the hospital was one of the most amazing experiences I have ever been witness to. Angie was wore out. She had been through a lot already that day and it was work just to get everything arranged so she could sit in a wheelchair. She was ready for a nap before leaving the room, but she was excited and knew whatever surprise was in store would be worth it.

The look on her face when she saw her pup again was that of pure joy, and Kona had the same look. He rarely was away from Angie and before she was admitted into the hospital, it was clear he could sense that something was wrong. The whole experience wasn't more than 15 minutes but the tears from all of us were tears of joy and hope and sadness all rolled into one. As I watched Angie's nurse, a woman in her twenties, about the same age as Ang, tear up it hit me what an impact Ang was having on others. Here she was on the beginning of this journey, impacting people she had just met with her kindness, her excitement for life, and her positive outlook. It started to become clear to me that Ang was exactly where she needed to be, that throughout all this craziness, God was using her and that she was fulfilling the purpose of her life.

John's surprise for Angie, a visit from Kona at the hospital.

CHAPTER 5

Shower and Stir-Fry

CARINGBRIDGE POST
by Angela Hazel, March 18, 2017

Hi everyone! It's back to me, Angie, typing tonight so I might stick to a short post as it's hard to hold my strength to type on my own. But unfortunately, I can't blame grammatical errors on anyone but myself when I'm doing the typing and not just the talking.

Today started out rough with an abnormal heart rate that lead to discussion of an EKG at 3 a.m. Thankfully, both the nurse and doctor felt it was unnecessary after reviewing the strip and decided to forgo the EKG. My Mom tackled giving me a shower this morning for the first time since Monday (I know, stinky). I evidently had gotten some sponge baths, but I was too weak for anyone to wash my hair, so I dealt with walking around like I dunked my head in a vat of oil olive as long as I could stand it. My Mom did amazing, but the shower really wiped me out and I felt pretty nauseated from all the activity. After a nice snooze, I was feeling better and ready to party with my visitors.

Labs are looking good, staying pretty steady. The doctor ordered extra potassium, but other than that, they looked normal.

I got to see many visitors today, include my aunt, uncle and cousins that drove 10 hours from Illinois to see me for just a day. They're amazing, and I'm so happy they could make it out!

I also got an amazing gift from some very special friends that live far away. A personalized pillow of my Kona dog! Cutest gift ever! I was awake and alert today to the point that I ate a homemade stir fry, a banana, some mashed potatoes and steamed veggies, and some crackers! This is a huge accomplishment as yesterday I couldn't even stomach the thought of food. Hopefully I'm back to following my own advice as a dietitian and get my appetite back enough to build up my strength!

Again, I'm feeling so much love with the "No One Fights Alone" picture that so many of you have shared on Facebook. The response is overwhelming! I love you all and thank you again for all the prayers that are being said for me and my family.

Angie's dog, Kona, wearing a sign of the No One Fights Alone logo that quickly spread across Facebook.

Jerry's Perspective

Faced with the reality of the situation, we eventually made the decision, as a family, to start calling in close family and friends to see her. We didn't know if she would survive the hospital stay and wanted her and those who love her to have *one more time*. One more conversation, one more hug, one more *I love you*.

So often we think of cancer as a death sentence, especially a diagnosis like Angie's. I never thought of it that way. I always thought of it as an opportunity that most people never have. Here she was knowing that she was up against insurmountable odds and she had the opportunity to do everything *one more time*. So many people kept flashing through my mind, so many accidents and unexpected deaths. So many people that wished they had one more time, five more minutes, and that is exactly what she was given with her cancer diagnosis. Exactly what *our family* was given. She was not ripped from our lives in an instant. She was given the chance to fight and to make her peace with this life.

In my mind, that started with being surrounded by everyone that she was closest to and who loved her the most. Those calls were hard, letting family know the severity of the situation. It was amazing to me how almost everyone dropped what they were doing and came at a moment's notice. It didn't matter that we struggled yearly to find time to get together as an extended family. Suddenly nothing else mattered and the only thing worth doing was making the trip to SD, to see Ang, and to be with us.

Having our extended family around helped me tremendously, especially my Aunt and Uncle from Minnesota. One night I came back from the hospital late with Dad, it was dark when we walked into my parent's house. My grandparents (my Mom's Dad and bonus Mom), and aunt and uncle were already there. They had brought all the kids there earlier in the evening, their two kids a good distraction for my three. I remember just losing it in the kitchen. My Dad and I explaining the severity of the situation, the last-ditch effort Ang had with this chemo to buy her more time. The likelihood that even if it worked, it would only be gaining time, not a cure.

And then, here comes my daughter, Aleigha, and her cousin from the living room with tears in their eyes.

"Is Angie going to die?"

We had thought all of the kids were asleep. I didn't realize they heard us. I felt a tremendous amount of guilt over speaking too loud, us having to explain this to not only my daughter, but also her cousin. I was planning on being honest with Ally when the time came, but I was not expecting it to be late at night and with company. I was not expecting it to be on a night when I couldn't keep it together.

But we talked. I told her Angie was fighting and the doctors were doing everything they could and that no one knows when anyone is going to die. The best thing we could do was pray. I was grateful that there were other adults to help me through this. Although I was saddened to see their daughter have to go through this pain with Ally, I was so thankful Ally had someone close to her age and that they could help each other comprehend.

We have an amazing family support system, but a tremendous community support system rallied overnight. Within hours of Angie's first CaringBridge post, a Facebook profile picture in her honor was popping up everywhere. It said, "No One Fights Alone! Team Angie." Very quickly we had people reaching out to see how they could help, even starting fundraising efforts within the first couple days of her hospital admission. While we were so grateful for the support and prayers, everything seemed to be moving so fast. We were so overwhelmed with wrapping our heads around what was happening that we couldn't fathom fundraising or other needs at that point. Everything felt out of control, it was all too much at once.

FAITH OVER FEAR

Once we had a couple days to grasp what was occurring and were able to have a couple of somewhat clear moments to discuss as a family and even a little with Ang, we realized that we needed to get ahead of everyone to maintain Angie's wishes. Ang never wanted to be thrown into the limelight. She started the CaringBridge site with a lot of hesitation, and only decided to move forward with it so her family and friends could hear the info straight from the source. She was very cautious of what she wrote and how she wrote it. Her inner control freak was coming out and it was impossible to please as everything was completely out of control.

Once family started arriving and we had a few free moments to discuss the plan going forward, we decided to create a Go Fund Me page for Angie and also to create t-shirts as a family, so they would be a design Ang would be proud of and would really speak to the situation. One night, I sat around the table with my cousins, a couple of my aunts and two of my grandmas brainstorming t-shirt ideas. We browsed Pinterest and Amazon finding all sorts of witty slogans for fighting cancer.

Cancer started the fight, I'm going to finish it!

Dear Cancer, you picked on the wrong woman!

Hope, Fight, Cure

A million designs, none of which seemed to fit. How do you create a shirt that rallies support, but more importantly rallies faith?

Finally, there it was *"Faith tells me that no matter what lies ahead, God is already there."* It was perfect.

For the front, we decided on, *"I'm realistic. I expect miracles."* We chose this because we wanted people to understand this wasn't a Stage 1 breast cancer diagnosis, where there are great odds at defeating cancer. This would take a true divine miracle, one that only God could provide.

When Angie and John saw the design, they requested that *"Faith Over Fear"* be added to the sleeve. It had become their new mantra, little did we know at the time, it would soon become the basis for which all of us would now live our lives.

Cassy's Perspective

My sister was driving me nuts! Not Angie, the other one, Negative Nancy. How can we be so different from each other? I've always looked up to Jessy, she fit the oldest role perfectly. She has so many characteristics that I admire, yet her outlook on how to treat Angie's diagnosis was so polar opposite of mine. I heard her speak of Angie's final wishes, quality of life, last goodbyes etc. so many times and thought where is your faith? I felt like she had applied for a position on the hospital's palliative care team and forgot to tell us. Is this how my parents felt? I understood Angie had stage 4 cancer, I understand it's been spreading like wildfire and they don't know where it stemmed from, I know what the doctors have said but this is OUR SISTER! If we don't have faith she can fight longer than just a couple weeks how the hell is she supposed to believe it?

I wasn't giving up, not without a fight. I wasn't going to be the one to tell people to come say their goodbyes. What kind of impact would that have on Angie, her knowing that we all gave up? The thing that was driving me crazy the most about my sister was deep down she was right. She's always right. Ugh, I hate that. I could see where she was coming from, who wouldn't want that opportunity to say all the things to those they loved most before they were gone?

In my mind, I still was just hopeful they could figure SOMETHING out, buy her more time. Heck, she was even drinking my pumped breastmilk to boost her immune system. When I asked her if she wanted to, she didn't even hesitate. Angie, more than anyone, realized the benefits that came from breast milk. Anything I could do to help her recover from chemo and feel better faster, I would do.

I knew Ang loved having visitors, but I could see in her eyes she knew why they were there. She was taking it all so well, but I wondered if it was more out of politeness than acceptance. I kept waiting for her to have a freak out moment, throw things, scream, but she didn't. God was holding on to her, telling her He was with her. Her strength was beautiful and powerful. We, as a family, were so unbelievably proud.

Cinter's Perspective

After three days of Angie being out of sorts, unable to finish her sentences, brush her teeth, repeating herself over and over, either sleeping or incredibly restless, Angie finally started to settle down. Out of town family came pouring in, it was wonderful to have all the support.

John's Perspective

The outpouring of support rings loud: meals, visits, messages of support. I could go on for days about how taken aback and appreciative I hope I've become from this experience. Never a day where myself or Angie weren't thankful for something or someone. Seeing her reading cards in the hospital; it would usually start with excitement, "I haven't seen them since…" or, "This is the person that I was telling you about at…" type of comments. Every finish was filled with tears, love, and appreciation from her. Angie had cancer everywhere it could spread to, but her heart was immune to the disease. We were all very thankful to survive the prior week and you could almost sense a small breath of fresh air within the group. There was still plenty of fight and battle to be had, but we still had Angie.

CHAPTER 6

Good Dietitian/Bad Dietitian

CARINGBRIDGE POST
by Angela Hazel, March 21, 2017

Well, I'm either a crappy chemo patient or a crappy dietitian. I have been trying to get meaningful calories in me the past week or so by sticking to smoothies, fruits, raw vegetables, and sneaking in some of my "favorites" like pizza and pasta, but yet my appetite has fallen greatly, and I've lost about 19 lbs. total (this includes bulking up an additional 8-14 lbs. in water weight from the fluid on my lungs and coming back down after draining them). Yesterday was a bad eating day, and I threw up EVERYTHING I tried to eat including cantaloupe, cucumbers, graham crackers and even water. I finally got a couple slices of apple settled at the end of the night.

Now I know you all didn't subscribe to my CaringBridge to read a food journal (and not even a good food journal at that, more of a list of foods I know longer ever want to see on my plate again), so I do have some good reason for telling you all of this. Yesterday was a step back in the pain management and nutrition outlook areas, but today we came leaps and bounds forward. I had constant, piercing pelvis and spine pain (two areas of the bone where my lesions were very predominant) that had me seeing stars all day, and the nausea could have easily gone hand-in-hand with my pain. Late yesterday afternoon after an MRI and trying to get ahead of my pain, the care team added a steroid back to my regimen and the bone pain anything but disappeared! The steroid is also likely to help with the nausea, but the doctor put me on an IV anti-emetic that allowed me to eat today! The bad dietitian in me was craving everything but healthy foods, but I kept down ham and cheese Hot Pockets, Dorito chips, gummy fruit snacks, and chocolate milk like a champ! High five for me!

CARINGBRIDGE POST

I came off of a great night of sleep after getting the pain managed, and rather than waking up every 1 1/2 hours, I slept 4 hours at a time! I'm sure my Mom/John feel like they have a newborn they're looking after as they have been staying at the hospital with me nightly! Hopefully on John's shift tonight I can sleep just as well! My labs looked great this morning, allowing me to come off of some of the medications I needed to keep my electrolytes in check. We also looked at this really general, non-specific but "best news we can see at this point" LDH value that shows just the general tumor presence in the body. My value upon admission was around 600, falling to 350 over the weekend and 277 today, which is within normal limits! While it doesn't mean much, it at least gives us hope that my body is fighting this nasty trick! My CBC panel is still reacting as they would expect based on the stage of chemo phase I'm on. My temperature has stayed normal lately, but we're still limiting visitors to keep my exposure low and taking precautions with masks.

Today my sister came up to the hospital to cut my hair. I've been told my hair will fall out 10-14 days after chemo, so we did a "pre-cut" and chopped off 6 inches, and man is it cute! I should have done this a while back! We have a wig appointment tomorrow to consult for a hopefully-not-anything-like-Donald-Trump hairpiece. I have high hopes! I'm a dry shampoo lover at heart, so not having to deal with my messy mop and throwing on a wig in the morning sounds like a sweet plan to me! I also will have a skin consult and get some scarves, etc., which is great because my face has been incredibly itchy lately from the treatment (any suggestions?). It will be a tough day as I can't imagine many women would be comfortable with losing all their hair, but it will be a good ease into the transition and just another step in the process. And every day I wake up bald is another day I get to at least wake up, right?

I keep returning to how grateful and humbled I am by the love and support I feel from everyone lately, but I can't express enough thankfulness to show my sincere love. I am in awe. For example, a coworker showed me an assignment from her daughter asking for a wish for a friend, in that her Mom's friend would get better from cancer. My Mom's best friend's son lost a daughter to cancer about 5 years ago, and his younger son offered to donate some of his birthday money to me to help me with my cancer because his sister had cancer and knew how hard it would be on me. This child has never even met me, and already has such a big heart and humble spirit that he was willing to share his BIRTHDAY GIFTS with me to cheer me up. God is love, and God is HUGE.

The cards, the well wishes, the prayers and the above and beyond extreme offerings of irreplaceable things has been so incredible to see. Words cannot describe how lucky I feel just to have an amazing and far-stretching community caring for me.

Cassy, Angie and Jessy during Round 1 of Angie's Chemo.

Cassy's Perspective

Being the cosmetologist in the family, naturally, left the task of cutting Angie's hair in my lap. I had dozens of customers come through the salon I had worked in over the years with some form of cancer proudly showing the little wisps of hair growing back. Telling their own battle story, sharing tears with them and being so grateful they had fought hard and beat cancer.

As I cut Angie's hair I wondered, "would this be the last time I'd ever be doing this?" In a few short days she'd be picking out wigs and scarves with a brave face and then silently her hair would fall from her head strand by strand. Would it ever grow back? Probably not.

Doing Angie's hair was something we did almost every time we were together. She went from being over anal and fussy in my early days to learning to trust me and would just say "do whatever you want." It was our time to sit and talk one on one. It was just a huge reminder while I cut her hair what a huge impact this sickness was having on her life.

The day came for her to go to the hospital's salon to pick out her wig. Jes, Mom and myself went for moral support. We tried to make light of it best we could and in true Angie fashion she knew exactly what she wanted. The woman helping us was very kind and I thought how many women has she had sit in her chair, weak, nauseated, making decisions I can guarantee not a single one wanted to make. How many made it into a "girls day" like us, trying to make the best of a crummy situation or cried through the whole appointment? How many dreams had she seen that wig crush the moment it was placed on that patient's head? The diagnosis was hard, the pain was hard, the nausea was hard, watching your friends and family hold back tears as to not make you feel worse was hard, but so was this. Why did cancer have to be so selfish?

Cinte's Perspective

The outpour of love and encouragement from everyone was absolutely amazing and unbelievable. My Dad and bonus Mom had basically moved here to help with everything. My Mom and step-Dad were there whenever we needed them and even when we didn't know what we needed. All the grandparents, aunts, uncles and many cousins were checking in daily either by visit, call or text. I seriously didn't think about anything except Angie's comfort and care. John's family also rallied around, helping everyone, especially John as they knew his needs best. We were so thankful for all the support.

The God Things kept pouring down. There was no way of denying them for what they were. "Faith Over Fear" and "Team Angie" was popping up everywhere from Facebook posts and profile pictures, to painted storefront windows and car windows in our small hometowns, purple ribbons everywhere. Our neighbor disked Angie's name into a field near our home. Her name could be read from the highway and prayers were sent up by friends and strangers who traveled by. Food was constantly brought to the house. It was amazing to see the entire community lifting our family up. Knowing my family was taken care of, I was able to focus on Angie. It takes a village.

The one time I went home during the first hospital stay, I got a glimpse of the community support Russ and the girls were seeing daily and was amazed by it all. However, the moment I walked into the house, I fell apart. I cried thinking that Angie may never come home again. I was so filled with anxiety that I left before dawn the next morning to head back to the hospital, needing to squeeze in every moment with her even if it meant only to watch her sleep. All the time I was away from her I was praying to God and thanking Him for everyone's input in our lives, but still unable to pray, "Thy will be done." Knowing this was wrong, as I wasn't putting my whole trust in Him but I could not let go.

◆

Jerry's Perspective

Often during a quiet moment in between home life, work life and hospital life, my mind would land on my Mom. Since that first call from Angie, she had been at her side or at the very least with her phone in her hand ready to stop whatever she was doing to rush to her again. My heart broke for her as I watched her pray over Angie's hospital bed each day and my mind constantly flashed back to three years prior, when I was doing the same for my child.

Just before he turned four months old, my son Conrad contracted RSV. During a follow-up appointment with the pediatrician, we were directed to go to the hospital. Within an hour of getting admitted, several doctors and nurses rushed into his room and decided to move him to the PICU immediately.

Conrad was born with some kidney concerns. At this point in his short life, he had already been hospitalized twice for UTI/ kidney infections and was being followed by both a urologist and a nephrologist. We were no strangers to this hospital or to procedures being done to our little baby, but this time was different. This was the PICU, the place where *critically* ill kids come. The place where things move quickly and urgently, and decisions must be made immediately to help these kids, and that day my Conrad was one of these kids.

A high flow oxygen cannula was placed on Rad. His oxygen levels improved, but he continued to breathe too fast, and it was tiring him out. His eyes were red and bloodshot. It was obvious he was struggling to breathe. I kept looking into his eyes and rubbing his arms and belly trying to calm him down, but his eyes just became more glazed over and his breathing would not slow. The PICU staff was constantly by his side. For hours, the doctor checked on him every 20 minutes, each time telling me "I'll give him a little longer," trying to offer me hope that Conrad would recover on his own yet explaining to me that if he continued to struggle, he would need

◆

additional medical help with a ventilator.

I had been sitting next to Conrad's bed for hours, yet the time flew by in 20-minute increments. I held my breath each time the doctor entered, praying he would see improvement but knowing full well Conrad was barely able to handle breathing on his own. The doctors had given Conrad several hours to try to stabilize his breathing, but it was just too much for his little lungs and for fear that he would not be able to breathe at all if he got too exhausted, they decided to intubate him. Despite being fully present for every conversation, it hit me like a ton of bricks.

By this time my husband, Kyle, made it up to the hospital. I don't think either of us realized the heavy reality of the situation until the doctor explained step by step how they were going to help Conrad by intubating him. He explained the ventilator would do the breathing for Conrad because his lungs were too sick. This would give Conrad the chance to rest and combat the RSV. He explained he wanted to "secure the airway" before Conrad absolutely could not breathe on his own. I knew in the back of my mind what being intubated meant. Having the breathing tube, being in a medically induced coma to allow the machine to breathe for him. But as the doctor explained this out loud, I began to cry and cry. This is my baby, and they are going to place all these foreign objects in him and pump him so full of meds that he sleeps for *days*.

He asked us to say what we wished to Conrad and then leave the room while they intubated him and placed a central line for the medications Conrad would need. This was one of the hardest things I have ever had to do in my life. I hugged my little baby that I had given birth to just 15 weeks earlier and told him he had to go to sleep for a few days, so his little body could fight the bad bugs. I knew I would not see his cute smile or hear his little baby talk or the big belly laugh that he had just started doing for *days*. I knew I would be unable to hold him and rock him to comfort him. I knew there was even a good chance he would not open those bright blue eyes during this time.

The doctor came out to the family room to bring us back to Conrad's room once the procedure was complete. There was our Rad, so small in the big hospital crib, hooked up to a big blue machine that was breathing *for him*. There were monitors on every side of him with different foreign numbers and squiggly lines that I would become all too familiar in how to decipher. It was hard to see that it was our little boy underneath all the tubes and wires.

Another x-ray confirmed the doctor's suspicion that part of his right lung had collapsed. Our Conrad was fighting with every piece of him to keep his lungs working yet looking at him in that big hospital crib, he finally looked calm after hours of strained red eyes and struggling for breath. He was finally getting the rest he needed.

For the next 10 days, I lived in that hospital room. I rarely stepped foot outside, unless it was to shower or grab a quick bite to eat. I sat next to his bed for hours, just silently praying that God would save my baby.

As the week went on, Conrad was continuing to have a hard time keeping his oxygen level up. At one point there was discussion about him getting close to max ventilator settings and the possible necessity of moving to an oscillator, a stronger type of ventilator if he reached that max. The doctor said with the path Conrad was taking so far, he appeared to be one of those kids that is likely to get even worse before he starts the climb to get better. They were concerned he could have a hole in his heart and ordered an echocardiogram.

During the time it took this tech to do the echocardiogram, I kept thinking, "what if they find something now that was missed during my pregnancy now that they are doing this test directly on him instead of in utero? What if he is suddenly thrown into open heart surgery next?" My mind was everywhere.

His echocardiogram came back without issue and since there was no hole in his heart causing the problem, the doctors continued their pursuit of how to best treat Conrad. In addition to the struggles with ventilator settings, it was a constant struggle to find the right balance of sedation drugs for him. Conrad was becoming more alert and harder to keep sedated as he got used to the meds, which resulted in him trying to breathe around the machine, making his body work harder and not giving him the rest he needed to heal.

A continuous VEC drip, a paralyzing sedation drug, was added to his IV. This was very difficult for me to see because when he did not have the VEC, he wiggled enough to let me know he was there. The vent monitor showed he started his breaths and the vent helped him finish the breath and do it at the right speed but when he had the paralytic, he could not move anything, so the vent did all his breathing for him. The doctors believed he was fighting the ventilator too much from within, which was not allowing his lungs to heal. I understood what they were trying to accomplish but all I saw on the vent monitor was red lines showing that the machines were doing everything for my little boy.

I spent so many hours just holding his limp little hand just thanking God for bringing this little boy into our lives and begging, pleading, and bargaining for more time with him. We were just getting to know him. He was the addition to our family we never knew we needed. We could not bear the thought of life without him.

By day five, additional fluid on Conrad's lungs was creating a problem. He became extremely swollen and puffy everywhere. It was so sad to see my baby now physically transformed as he swelled up. All his adorable little baby fat rolls disappearing into swollen legs and neck.

That day they were working hard on adjustments to the ventilator settings and his doctor determined he needed to find out what Rad was capable of doing and get a better idea of the pressure he needed. This could only be done, by taking him off the ventilator (leaving the breathing tube still intact) and using the bag to manually pump air into the breathing tube for just a few minutes. It didn't take long for the doctor to do this but once they had him back on the vent he was very red in the face and looked like he had tears under his eyes. I asked if he was OK and they said, "Yes, he is just mad from all the manipulation." From a mommy's perspective, it sounded like he was crying on the inside and because he is under the sedation and paralytic we couldn't see it. It absolutely broke my heart. I knew they were pumping him full of meds to keep him from remembering it all and to keep him calm and sedated, but they said on more than a few occasions how he went through the sedation drugs like candy and he is maxed out most of the time on the dosages. It just killed me to think that he was upset under all those meds. More than anything, I just wanted to hold him and comfort him.

With the issues of all the fluid, a renal panel now needed to be done daily to check his kidney function, which further increased my worry. So far, his kidneys had not been harmed by him having RSV, but what if that changed? What if this ruined whatever functionality he had left, and he needed dialysis? My mind constantly spun with scenarios.

It became so difficult to see him have continuous bumps in the road to recovery. I just kept praying he would turn that corner and start the climb back up and I became so jealous when I heard other babies in the PICU crying at the top of their lungs. I just wanted my baby back.

The next couple days showed slight improvement, they were able to wean him off the paralytic sedation. He grasped my finger tight and looked right into my eyes instead of through me. He was getting there, and I held on to my hope and faith that everything would be OK.

On day eight, his four-month-old birthday, the doctor determined Conrad had suddenly contracted a secondary infection. Every time he took a step forward, he took two steps back. It became impossible and faith was so hard to hold on to.

The right antibiotics helped him turn back around and when the doctors saw a window of improvement, they pushed Conrad off the ventilator on day ten. Once he was settled on high-flow oxygen I was finally able to hold my baby and the sweet smile he gave me was the reassurance I needed to know that God answered my prayers.

For the following nine days, Conrad slowly improved. He gradually weaned from high flow oxygen to regular oxygen, to room air. He went through withdrawals from the morphine and versed sedation drugs and would cry uncontrollably for hours. It further broke my heart to see my child go through withdrawals the same as a drug addict does, even though I fully understood how necessary those drugs were at the time to keep him alive. Everything was a challenge. My chubby baby since birth forgot how to nurse, and IVs and a feeding tube had to remain while he re-learned how to eat. Eventually, Conrad overcame every challenge in his own time frame. God brought us through that incredibly difficult time.

And now, thinking of Angie and reflecting upon Conrad's trials, my heart just broke for my Mom as three years ago, I had a small glimpse of the hell she was going through now. I knew what it felt like to plead for my baby's life, to spend hours just holding their hand waiting for a miracle. I knew what it was like to have your mind racing with a thousand possible scenarios every time a new test, lab or procedure was done. I knew what it was like to see your baby physically transformed from an illness. I knew what it was like to pray every moment for your child to be saved so you can continue to be part of their life. It hurt me so much to know she was feeling that pain and more.

CHAPTER 7

Faith Over Fear

CARINGBRIDGE POST
by Angela Hazel, March 24, 2017

Faith Over Fear has been the theme during the past few weeks that have flew by in a whirlwind. I think everyone that has been close to/involved in this process can attest to the fact that the longest nights in the world can turn into the longest days, and yet all of a sudden Tuesday turns into Friday in the blink of an eye. Having faith and courage to fight the unknown has been a struggle, but fear is not an option.

For example, I have gotten great sleep the past couple nights until the early morning, when all of a sudden, I wake up to a tornado of activity with my nurse saying my fever has spiked and we need to start the mandatory procedures that follow a fever spike in the middle of the night–chest x-ray, blood culture, urine samples, antibiotics, infectious disease doctor consultations, the whole she-bang. My calm waters turned into a tumultuous sea in the matter of minutes. It's easy to feel fearful in this situation, but a great nurse filled with patience and a prayer sent up to God smoothed the seas. Thankfully, my doctor said that fevers are a "normal" part of the process with my immune system basically wiped out, and we just need to do our best to keep traffic low in my room, wash in and out, and rest through it.

The good news is everything is pointing in the right direction. The chest x-ray is clear, EKG is normal, electrolytes are being balanced and my white count/platelets/RBCs are behaving as expected. They also began me on TPN because I just can't keep up orally with my nutrition. More lines, but I'm very grateful because this takes some of the stress off of me to try to make myself eat when I'm in pain/

have no appetite.

Not the funny, lighthearted post I wanted to make tonight, but it's been a tough day with some obstacles. Funnily enough, I had gotten a sweet message from a friend the other day saying she would pray for me to overcome hurdles this week and that is exactly what I needed! Her intuition was impeccable.

Speaking of prayers and love, again, the response is overwhelming. From t-shirt sales, donations, gifts, I can't describe my gratitude. How lucky am I to have such a loving community and support network?

♡Angie

Carter's Perspective

The doctors, nurses, and our village around us, everyone in our support network, were helping in their own way to make things more comfortable for Angie and easier for the rest of us.

Angie made a comment about her skin being itchy, and skincare products showed up in the mail.

We needed extra prayers, and prayer chains across the country lifted her name.

The nurses not only did their job but brought in extras like essential oils to help with anxiety and sleeplessness. They truly cared about their patients 24 hours a day, not just the hours they were on the clock. We found ourselves surrounded by a whole new family while at the hospital.

It was a God Thing every time someone that we knew from the past was back in our path again. Often, we hadn't seen these people for years, but now they were a familiar face that was able to work their specialty to bring comfort to Angie. Sometimes it was just seeing someone in the hallway, sometimes they were staff, sometimes they crossed our path during a quick trip to the store, always they were exactly what we needed at that moment. Strangers would stop us to ask about the quote on the Team Angie shirts we wore and tell us how much they loved it and that they would pray for our Angie. Sometimes they even wanted to know how we knew Angie because they had heard of her story, and even though they had never met her, they were already praying.

So often people wonder when there is a tragedy what they can do to help, the truth is anything and everything done matters if, for even a moment, it brings a smile to someone's face and comfort to their heart.

John's Perspective

Let's talk hospital! Now I start this off with the most important factor, the staff. What an amazing staff they were. Every nurse and doctor we dealt with were truly great people, whenever we needed help or had questions they were patient, willing, and would do everything in their power to help. Doing things that weren't in any job description I can assure you. Part of me couldn't help but think these nurses, who in many cases, appeared to be similar in age to Angie, couldn't put themselves in her shoes. Another point that truly amazes me about Angie is how courteous she was to each person that walked into her room. Always remembering each doctor and nurse by name. Carrying on a conversation from previous days or stays. She enjoyed them, and they enjoyed her back.

I think about the earlier statement about patience and Angie owning it, myself not so much. I can tell you how many times I've been rude or inconsiderate for waiting in a line longer than I felt was appropriate. This girl has been stuck on a bed and never took that frustration out on anyone. She kept her faith, at times questioned why, but always composed herself with grace throughout the situation.

If I ever become a multi-billionaire, my life mission will be to invent, invest, and distribute a fold-out bed solely built for hospitals! I've had two jobs since college, both that require hotel travel and stays on a regular basis. It used to be easy to complain about being in a bed that wasn't yours, pillows that weren't ideal, forgetting a charger, etc. I can tell you since my experience, I complain much less about being in that environment. Living out of a hospital for days (or at times weeks) at a time, is a miserable time. The hospital beds were rough for sleeping but given the situation, sleep wasn't going to be guaranteed or a top concern either. I'll mention the food, and I understand it's not an easy task to plan for that many people, but let's just say we had memorized a food map in a 4-mile radius pretty quickly! I mention these challenges half-jokingly but those things wear a person down slowly.

Jerry's Perspective

Ang was constantly on my mind. Part of me ached for people to ask how she was doing and for them to genuinely be looking for an honest response. People asking about her didn't upset me. It didn't make me suddenly get sad. It didn't suddenly remind me that she had cancer. I was always sad, always upset, always thinking about how my sister was fighting for her life. The other part of me got to a point where I was torn about even talking to other people because they just didn't understand.

When people first started finding out about Angie's cancer, the first question was always "what kind is it?" A response of "Cancer of Unknown Primary" or "they do not know", got a cockeyed look every time. It is unfathomable that in this day and age, there is not a name for every illness. People assumed she had bottom of the line health care and start rattling off doctor recommendations.

"You know so-and-so had cancer. They were in really rough shape. They saw Dr. Anybody at Any Other Hospital and look at them today!"

"What kind of cancer did they have?"

Leukemia.

Breast cancer.

Colon cancer.

Hodgkin's.

Thyroid.

Take your pick, it doesn't matter. All of these people that were in "really rough shape" had a name for their cancer. With a name for the cancer comes a plan. Ang still didn't have a name for her cancer. Her doctors didn't have a proven plan to defeat it. No one did.

By this point multiple oncologists and multiple pathology teams were working to figure out what she had. Her biopsies were being looked at from several angles. She had consults with doctors and pathology teams in Kansas City, Sioux Falls, San Diego, Grand Rapids and Rochester. The best of the best were stumped. Here we were, weeks into the constant testing, well into her first round of treatment and her cancer still did not have a clear name. When all other options were exhausted, the best conclusion her doctors could come up was still that her cancer was likely a sarcoma which possibly originated in the connective tissue. It doesn't much matter the name, it was the devil in every sense.

I was trying so hard to be positive for Ang, but I was stuck in the limbo between the hospital, where time stands still, and everything is focused on Angie's care, and the real word of a being a Mom, working full time, and handling the day to day.

Each night, I would put my kids to bed, usually reading them a book and laying in their bed listening to their stories of the day as they drifted off to sleep. And almost every night when it got quiet, right before they were sound asleep, my mind started drifting off. Memories of our childhood, thoughts questioning why this was happening, prayers for hope and strength to make it through. The tears silently ran down my face as I tried to hold them back, afraid I would wake up and worry my kids further.

There were already plenty of bedtimes that had to answer hard questions.

Why is Angie sick?

How did she get cancer?

Is her hair going to fall out?

Why can't she play? Why does she cough so hard? Why can't I bear-hug her?

Is she going to die?

And each time I would answer as honestly as I could. My kids knew plenty of people who had defeated cancer, Grandpa Ray, Uncle Marky, Uncle Dougie. But also others who had lost the battle, Grandma's friend, the little girl Ally went to daycare with years ago, the high schooler from our small town. They knew it could go any direction.

I couldn't lie to them, but I didn't tell them everything, just bits and pieces broken down to their level. Breadcrumbs, leading them to pray, reminding them of how much Jesus loves them and Angie and our family because we believe. Teaching them about Heaven and that death wasn't the end and reminding them of the love of their Grandpa Ray who passed the year prior. Reminding them that God is the only one who knows the date anyone will go to Heaven. Explaining the doctors were working hard to help Angie any way they could. Never telling them that Angie might die, but never just brushing it all off as ok. They are very close to Angie, their Aunt Gigi. It needed to be recognized that they were struggling through this as much as the rest of us.

CHAPTER 8

Prayers Are Being Answered!

CARINGBRIDGE POST
by Angela Hazel, March 27, 2017

As everyone has seen, cancer has been all up and downs since the diagnosis first tumbled from my oncologist's mouth on March 10. I'm happy to say I've had so many more ups than downs lately, and I know that has to do with everyone out there praying for me. Physically, today was great! I went for a couple walks and walked further than I ever have before in the hospital (talking about almost making laps here, people!) and I had an awake afternoon to visit with family.

Emotionally it was a tough day at times as my hair finally has begun to fall out. I'm expecting Lifetime movie scene where I'm pulling out chunk after chunk straight from the side of my scalp, but it was much more graceful and quiet than that (at least so far). I've got my sister on shaving duty later this week, but my wig has already arrived and is just waiting for me to build up the courage to put it on again.

Again, physically things look good! White cell count is up, no fevers or other signs of infection, and weaning from the TPN tonight. I also get to lose the IV on my right arm and am working on the transition to pain patches vs the IV narcotics, so we can get rid of this PICC tomorrow following my port placement. Big things are happening here, people!

And everyone rejoice, the plan is for me to be released from the hospital on Wednesday or Thursday! Hallelujah, time for a home cooked meal and to see my puppy dog! I'll be staying at my parents' house of course and will have to run to Sioux Falls here and there for testing, but the plan is that I'll be home until my next round of chemo begins on April 10.

Angie's parents, surrounding her with love during Round 1.

Jerry's Perspective

With each CaringBridge update, more and more of Angie's personality started to come out. People who did not know her, but knew other family members, John's family, or a friend of a friend, started to see Angie's personality. They saw her wittiness, her sarcasm, her upbeat attitude and her fight. I loved hearing that people were reading her CaringBridge, that they looked forward to her updates and that she was providing them hope. Here was my sister, fighting for her life and *she was giving other people hope.*

At various points in her life, Angie really struggled with anxiety. The heaviness of trying to be perfect, tasks like driving through a thunderstorm or coming home late at night alone would be enough to shake her to her core at times. But here she was facing the battle of her life head on, staring the devil in the eyes and she held her head high and stood strong. It was evident in her writing and when in her presence that God was holding her.

It was amazing to see this rally that started out with family and friends grow quickly to envelop acquaintances and strangers through her CaringBridge following and for all of them to so deeply care about my sister, not just because they empathized or felt sorry for her but because they were falling in love with her. Her personality, her spirit, her faith. She was like a magnet, drawing people to her story and her fight and most importantly lighting a fire with her faith. God was using her.

John's Perspective

Angie's personality and some of her quirks are what I miss most about her. One aspect I will never forget is Angie with her screw on lids. Yes, I am talking about any lid that has to be screwed onto a liquid container. I remember during a road trip, Angie was drinking a Dr. Pepper 20 oz. bottle, when she had dropped the lid in between the car seat and the center console. Now I figured human nature is that a person sticks their hand down there and endlessly searches for the lid until they can locate it. Mind you, she is in the passenger seat, we had multiple hours left driving in this car, and she had only had a couple sips so this was a likely spill in the making! Angie put her hand down in the crevice, and within a 2-second unsuccessful swipe, determined it was gone forever! I was in disbelief. After a brief conversation, it was determined if I wanted that cap back on the bottle, it would be me finding it! So for the next couple miles, my right hand was blindly twisting and turning for a cap that was evading my fingers until I finally snagged it.

If you think one story is a fluke about a cap, and that I'm OCD about one incident (which I may still be a little OCD!), wrong! One morning soon after that story, I made breakfast after Angie had left for work. I went for the orange juice, and like any person, went to shake the juice to mix the contents and pulp. Wouldn't you know it, the next 20 minutes I was cleaning OJ that was spilled all over the kitchen. If you couldn't put together what happened, I will help you out further. Angie had some juice before she left for work, didn't like screwing lids on all the way, didn't screw this lid, when I shook the container OJ went in every nook-and-cranny the kitchen had to offer!

CHAPTER 9

Home

CARINGBRIDGE POST
by Angela Hazel, March 29, 2017

Today is discharge day! The doctor has made his rounds and labs look good, just waiting to remove my PICC and get the final clear all! I cannot express how lucky I feel to have had the care I did while at Avera. The doctors made multiple visits to my room daily, the case manager worked her tail off to get my files transferred as needed, and the nurses/techs were incredible. Many nurses went out of their way to care for me, making me essential oil blends to help me sleep and explaining processes to me multiple times that I just couldn't quite grasp during my confused stage of the journey. I cannot praise them enough.

Everyone's prayers, thoughts, incredible kindness and support is the strength I need to walk out of here today. There were times when I was first admitted where no one believed I would walk out of the hospital alive, but here I am! Praise God!

♡Angie

Jerry's perspective

The day Ang walked out of the hospital, we all breathed a sigh of relief. She survived. She made it through the first round. She defeated the odds when things looked impossible. She was given the gift of more time.

That sigh of relief provided hope. It was a reminder of the words the oncologist used at the beginning of her stay, "If anyone can defeat this it would be someone young and in perfect health ordinarily, someone like Angie."

In anticipation of Angie's arrival home to Mom and Dad's, the house was plastered with coloring pages from the kids, window paint with encouragement, even notes on the bathroom mirrors. Hand sanitizer was strategically placed throughout the house and signs were hung on every door reminding any visitors to wash their hands and kindly stay away if they had any sign of illness. We weren't taking any chances.

And for that brief moment in time, life went on, as normal as it could be. Everyone watched Ang like a hawk, accommodating her in any way possible, doing our best to protect her, and soak up every moment we had with her.

Cinter's Perspective

After the longest sixteen days ever, Angie was back home at our place again. I was excited for her but also scared. I tried to keep up on all the medications—when, why, and what they are for. It is easy to rely on the nursing staff and they are absolutely awesome at their job. They had something they didn't learn in class—compassion. That is the gift of God working.

At home, watching her be able to relax somewhere other than a hospital bed, where she could enjoy Kona and her nieces and nephews more freely was wonderful. I just wanted to make sure I was doing everything possible to keep her comfortable. Thanks to some generous people, Angie had a new adjustable air bed. This was such a necessity to help her with her breathing issues and pain. Simply saying thank you wasn't enough.

Coming home, also meant a little bit of normalcy. I walked away from two jobs at the beginning of March and never looked back. I was so fortunate there were people to pick up the pieces and keep things going for me until I was able to return.

One night, I went to work at the library and Russ was at home with Angie. John had gone back to Kansas City for a few days to catch up on work also. Russ called me, Angie is in pain, what should he do? Angie did very well with her meds but sometimes it was hard for her to think straight when she was in so much pain. I closed the library doors early, so grateful for small towns and the understanding the community had.

We all had our positions we fell into. They say it takes a village, and that is true. Thank God Russ was there for all the business stuff and the community updates. I went to town and cried when I saw all the storefront windows painted and Angie's name written in the field. When people came into the library, I wasn't very good at holding it together. It was a struggle to stay composed when I wasn't with Angie.

With her trip home also came losing her hair. With Angie's hair loss, Kona, her Goldendoodle, began shedding. This is the only time I have ever seen a loose hair on Kona. I seriously believe he was just as upset as everyone else and knew something was wrong with Angie as she wasn't her usual energetic self.

Angie had been mentioning that she wanted her hair shaved, she didn't want to wake up with big clumps of hair on her pillowcase. Cassy had brought the shaver out to our house, but it did not get done that day. When Angie decided it was time to get the job done, I was the only one home with her. I tried to shave her head for her, but I couldn't see through my tears. I knew it was only hair, and hair grows back, but all that kept flashing through my head was memories of all the times I brushed her hair or fixed her hair before school or church, all the times she got beautiful updos for proms or weddings. This was one of the hardest days for me since finding out her timeline. Angie was handling it like a champ, until it started taking too long. Then she got a little upset and wanted it done. John came home just in time to finish the job and bring her comfort in the way that only he knew how to do.

She was truly the most beautiful bald woman I know. There is something about her that just glowed.

John's Perspective

Angie chose to be strong for a good part of her treatment. There were moments when vulnerability showed, which is absolutely to be expected and likely a healthy behavior to exhibit. Topics of general faith, pain to the point of questioning why enduring the continual aching and overall discomfort was worth it. But a point that absolutely broke me internally was when she finally accepted and went through with cutting her hair. Such a pivotal point, and one that she deeply expressed as a concern early into the process.

It was symbolic of so many things to me, I only imagine to what extent it truly meant for her internally. Is it that you're finally admitting a disease? Does it mean you are losing a part of or the entire battle? Will you ever be able to grow hair again? To me, what it ultimately ended up doing was removing that "make-up" you're exposed to so much and to so many. Like I mentioned in the beginning, luckily for Angie, she had a smile that would light up a room, and facial features that many would perceive to make her a beautiful person. The make-up and being dolled up never was something Angie needed, it only enhanced what was already there. The haircut essentially removed all of the superficial features people so often put too much emphasis on during their daily routine. Yet she remained one of the most beautiful kind of people you could be. The change absolutely took some adjusting to be able to go out in public without her "shield" of hair. But when she would boldly step out without it, I would be so proud of her. In reflection, that's something I should have reminded her in every possible moment.

Cassy's Perspective

The day Angie got released from the hospital could not come fast enough. It was a day I know my Mom feared greatly might never happen. Walking into my parents' house that night was overwhelming and comforting all at the same time. Signs on the door reminding people to "scrub in," bottles and bottles of pills, and every inch of countertop space covered with food dropped off by loved ones. But she was home.

My family and I came over that night for supper, desperately needing some normalcy. I tried my best to block out the sanitizers and the pill bottles and just soak in time with my parents and sisters. We knew Ang had limited energy, but she was giving me her best effort to try to keep up. I had very high hopes for some good quality time before her next trip back to the hospital.

Again, that night there were mentions of me shaving her head, it was probably the third or fourth time she had asked me but for whatever reason it just didn't get done. Each time she'd say, "I think it's still ok, maybe tomorrow." I never pushed it knowing it'd be super emotional for the both of us. Thankfully when the time came my Mom and John were able to handle it. Typical Angie, one day she just made a decision and jumped in, no looking back.

CHAPTER 10

Birthday Week!

CARINGBRIDGE POST
by Angela Hazel, April 3, 2017

I didn't realize how much I wanted/needed to be at home until I got here, and now I can't imagine spending another 16 days in the hospital! I've been sleeping better, building strength, eating more and feeling more awake. My family is careful to make sure I'm not overdoing it (meaning yes, they baby me quite a bit!) and I can't show them enough love for what they've done for me. Everyone has gone out of their way to make sure I'm comfortable, from my cousins donating us an incredibly comfortable adjustable air mattress and frame to help with my breathing, to rearranging room and schedules, and even installing a shower chair for this weak old lady.

The few days I've been home have been filled with activity because (hold your breath), IT'S BIRTHDAY WEEK! My Dad's birthday was yesterday, my birthday is Wednesday and Aleigha's (my niece's) birthday is on Friday. On Saturday, John planned an awesome get together in Sioux Falls with friends and family from all over the country! There were a lot of happy tears, surprises, and even a beautiful three-layer cake that made the trip to SD all the way from Kansas City! Sunday was filled with celebration as well, including church, family pictures, a delicious meal and way too many presents at the farm. On Sunday, Cubby's in Brookings hosted an amazing fundraiser for me! Although I wasn't strong enough to go, I heard there was an INCREDIBLE turnout. I can't thank Cubby's and all my friends and family enough that came out for the support! (And the fact that you got to eat delicious sweet potato fries and drink the best berry mojitos in the Midwest makes me incredibly jealous.)

My doctors advised me to eat everything that sounds good, and trust me, I've been doing just that. No food is safe around me, I inhale it all. I'm working to get some pounds back on my frame in case chemo decides to kick my butt again with the taste changes, lack of appetite or difficulty swallowing like last time. With that said, I have a good feeling going into this next round of chemo on Monday. I feel stronger and healthier than I did when I was first admitted and have made a lot of progress with my breathing. We will find out more information on Friday when we return to the hospital for a CT scan to be sure the chemo is doing its job.

Despite the positivity of last week's post, one of the biggest struggles I've had is processing the fact that I am losing my hair. We decided to shave it last Friday morning because it was rapidly falling out and the night sweats I experience (12:00-3:00 every afternoon and 3:00 a.m. every day, for some odd reason) were making it nothing short of torturous to sleep. It was a good decision in the long run as I can tell the hair is falling out more aggressively now and I would have hated it to have chunks fall out in front of my friends and family this weekend, but it's been quite the adjustment. I've worn my wig when I've been out and about, but man alive does that make my head sweat too! The wig is much more voluminous than my normal hair, so I feel more comfortable with a headband or hat to cover up my roots and tame it down a bit. Adding together the already sweaty chemo head with the wig cap, no-slip headband, wig, and headband/hat and I am a hot, itchy mess after 10 minutes! Around home I've been experimenting with caps, turbans, scarves... but I think I still need to spend more time on YouTube perfecting all these styles before I'm ready to tackle the world in them. To be completely honest, it's hard for me to look at my bald head in the mirror because it catches me off guard each time. Imagine seeing the same image staring back at you each day for 25 years, only to change so dramatically one day you can't recognize yourself. Shock is the only word I can find to explain the feeling.

The hip/lower back pain are managed well, to the point where I actually feel normal (unless I dip it low, then definitely need help getting back up. Anyone have a Life Alert I could borrow?). The pain is concentrated in my right, upper chest, but no cough. An incredibly sweet neighbor who is a nurse stopped by this weekend to listen to my breathing due to the increase in pain, and I still sound very clear. I can't imagine my lungs are filling up again, so right now we're just trying to manage pain until I visit the doctor again on Friday. We'll try switching my pain medication tomorrow from oxycodone to morphine to see if that helps.

Kona has been my trusty sidekick all weekend, never leaving my side. He is such a snuggler, and I've loved every second of it! He's been so good staying out of trouble on the farm, and we've only had to give him one bath after a careless romp in the creek led to mud all the way up his legs and belly. He's just another reason to get this chemo done and discharged from the hospital quickly this time!

♥Angie

Angie, Aleigha, and Russ: The Birthday Buddies

Jenny's perspective

Birthday week is a very real thing in the Hazel family, and for those with birthdays that lie in that week, it is sacred.

Just like most every year, we gathered at our parents' for a birthday celebration on Sunday. Each year, my daughter, Aleigha, gets so excited for her birthday celebration with the Hazel side. She knows it's not just for her but also for Angie and Grandpa Russ and that Angie loves birthdays just as much as Aleigha does. In previous years, they have had coordinating cakes, Ally's favorite being the year they each had a Barbie cake, hers in pink frosting dress and Angie's in a purple one.

This year there was no coordinated cakes, for one thing Ally turned 11 and had somewhat outgrown a Barbie cake, but there was still plenty of good desserts, each birthday buddy picking their favorite. I will never forget singing that Happy Birthday song. All of us adults with tears in our eyes, trying to cover them up with happy smiles and off-key singing. Angie closing her eyes at the end, straining her face as she made the biggest wish ever when blowing out her candles.

Angie with Andrea and Julia, two of her closest friends since elementary school at the birthday party John threw for Angie.

Cinter's Perspective

Birthday week has always been a huge deal to Angie. She reverts back to when she was three years old and we pull out all the stops to help her celebrate. Plus John threw an absolutely beautiful birthday in Sioux Falls with all her friends that came from across the U.S. All the guys had shaved their heads, which was a beautiful gesture.

This group of friends had become part of the family, surrounding Angie with love, always wanting to do something to help but never interrupting our time with Angie. I have never met a group of nicer, more polite young adults ever.

Cassy's Perspective

The week of Dad, Angie and Ally's birthdays was like a free-for-all, no rules applied. We were cramming in as much as possible, knowing it was very likely going to be the last birthday we would have with Angie, although no one was saying it.

The birthday party at the farm was great but we could all feel the heaviness of it. Angie's friends on the other hand, seemed to do a much better job of cheering her up. I know she was nervous going into it as many of her friends had not seen her since before she was sick as some lived quite a distance away. She hadn't been feeling well on the way to Sioux Falls and in general just having a crummy day, she was self-conscious of her weight and hair loss and having so much attention focused on her and asked me a few times if she looked ok. But the second she walked in and saw all her friends and the extreme amount of love they poured into that party, her anxiety melted away.

She truly couldn't have found a more supportive and loving group of friends. These people had become such a large part of her life, I think she actually forgot she was sick for a couple hours. Laughter was the best birthday gift they could have given her. It was truly a beautiful moment to see all the effort John and their friends had put into it.

CHAPTER 11

"Ringing" In 26!!

CARINGBRIDGE POST
by Angela Hazel, April 7, 2017

As I'm sure many of you saw on Facebook, John proposed!! Words cannot describe how elated I am to be his fiancé, or how incredibly lucky I am to have found such a wonderful man. He has stuck by me through the roughest part of my life with such love and understanding...I just thank God every day for letting me love him.

As for the engagement story, I'll do my best but to be honest, I was so shocked and thrilled when it happened, I had to have John remind me of what words he even used! I'm pretty sure I blacked out when I saw him get down on one knee...and the rest is a blur! For my birthday, I wanted to be normal for a few hours. I asked that John and I had some alone time, because even though he has barely left my side throughout this process, we still haven't had much one on one time. We decided to go out for lunch and indulge in the greasiest, most delicious burger we could find (Phillips Diner, burger melt!). It was amazing. Just getting out of the house and eating a delicious meal would have been a perfect birthday too, just to feel like the old days again. Keep in mind, an hour drive to SF, parking a block away on a hill, and sitting at a restaurant for an hour can take all the wind out of my sails! We were walking back to the car and I mentioned I felt like I was turning 65, not 26, the way I was RELYING on him to help me up the incline on the sidewalk and how short of breath I was by the time we got back to the car.

My Mom surprised me by scheduling a birthday massage for later that afternoon, so we had a bit of time to kill. John suggested we stop by Falls Park since we were so close. I debated taking a painkiller after our walk but figured I could hold off until after the park (thank goodness I did or I may have fallen asleep in the car and spoiled the entire plan!). After a couple detours and getting only slightly lost, we got to the park and tackled a few more stairs to get up next to the water. Now, if you haven't been to Falls Park or even South Dakota in early April, let me tell you...not much has bloomed yet. It's pretty dreary, and all the trees are still in hibernation mode. We joked about how it fits my life right now... still beautiful with the waterfalls trickling down through the rocks, but the cancer just killing all the life out of the fluff of it all–no leaves, no green grass, no flowers, not even any fresh white snow!

This is the part where things get foggy. John turns to me and says, "Ang, you've have enough bad surprises this month and you deserve at least one good surprise on your birthday (and it definitely was that, an incredibly unexpected and wonderful surprise!)." And he got down on one knee and pulled out the most beautiful ring to ask me to be his wife! Of course, I bawled. And bawled and bawled. I didn't even say yes for the first five minutes because I couldn't get the word out! It was perfect, every bit of it. At that point, sensible John pulled hysterical Angie away from the water, so I didn't drop the ring in the water (again, if you don't know me very well I'm the most clumsy person in the world. It would not be a stretch to imagine me dropping a brand-new engagement ring into a waterfall).

So keep in mind, this man pulled out all the stops. He had nail polish in the car in case I wanted to paint my nails before I showed off my ring to my friends and family, tissues in his pocket, just everything! We couldn't toast to our engagement with a drink, so we got glass bottles of cream soda to cheers! It's crazy when I think of how I used to believe our engagement story would play out, but our perfectly imperfect day was exactly how WE as a couple needed it to be. I love this man more than anything in the world, and I can't imagine spending the rest of my life with anyone else. If he can love me through this time and sacrifice so much for me, he's definitely a keeper.

Angie Hazel is with John JP Kolbach.
April 5, 2017

A month ago, my family was told I may not live to see my 26th birthday due to the nasty aggressiveness of a very rare cancer taking over my body. This past month has been the most challenging of my life, and like always, John has been by my side every step of the way. Today, this selfless, amazing, perfect man asked me to be his wife. Not sure what that doc was talking about, but I think my 26th year will be my best yet and I wouldn't miss it for the world.

○ Love   💬 Comment

As posted on Facebook

John's Perspective

We were able to share some very fortunate events with Angie. Given we weren't guaranteed anything beyond that initial week, we were able to create so many lasting memories, most of which a proposal that was most likely long overdue if you ask either of our family or friends! I'll shoulder the blame on the cold feet part there, I've always been a late bloomer, ask my Mom—I was even a few WEEKS late during her pregnancy!

It's a fitting transitional topic to discuss how this sickness somehow brought all of Angie and my friends and family to just become one family. So much collaboration, selfless acts, and an overwhelming willingness to do whatever was necessary to strive for one common goal. This event brought me so much closer to so many good people, words would never be able to fully express my gratitude.

Cassy's Perspective

Angie is an incredibly easy person to love, it was no wonder John proposed. It was always more of a matter of when than if the engagement was going to happen.

Daydreams of rings, dresses, attendants and venues cross every girl's mind from the time they have that first real crush all the way until the words "will you marry me," come from their new fiancé's lips. Angie was no different, her wedding Pinterest board had grown exponentially over the years of dating John. Her and I spoke often of colors, bridesmaids and honeymoon destinations. Never in those daydreams though did she have cancer. Never did she worry if she could find a dress that would cover her port, or if her hair would grow back long enough to have me style it, would she be able to keep her nausea and pain under control enough to actually enjoy the day, plan a ceremony around chemo treatments and especially she didn't worry about not having enough time to plan a wedding. However, those were the circumstances she was in.

The moment John asked her to marry him though all those dreams and worries became insignificant. He asked. It meant more to Angie than I think anyone could comprehend, I saw it all over her face the evening of her birthday when she flashed a ring in my face and announced their news. She didn't need a gorgeous gown, she was glowing. In that moment, everything was perfect, John showed Ang just how much love he had for her. That he was in this for better or worse, in sickness and in health, until death do them part.

Jenny's perspective

Ang has always loved her birthday. The world pretty much needs to stop and celebrate with her, and this year was no exception. There was plenty to celebrate between her discharge from the hospital, finally starting to feel a little better, and her and John's engagement. We were all beyond elated.

It finally looked like everything was making sense. It appeared the treatment was working or at least stabilizing things. She had the most beautiful, inspiring engagement story, she had tremendous support from family and friends. She was an incredible speaker and storyteller. It seemed like the stars were aligning and that this struggle was just going to be part of her life story, one chapter in a long book. Maybe Cassy was right, maybe I needed to have more faith. Maybe Ang would be the modern-day biblical miracle we were all praying for.

For this moment, life was good.

Cassy's Perspective

One of her biggest dreams came true...John asked her to marry him. Like I said before, he always knows how to make her feel the best.

CHAPTER 12

We've Got A Plan!

CARINGBRIDGE POST
by Angela Hazel, April 8, 2017

Thank you everyone for the well wishes and happy birthday love! It's been overwhelming reading all of the posts and seeing all the support we have as we continue on to the next stage of our life together!

Yesterday was a big appointment day as I am sure many remember from my post a few days ago. We went to Avera in the early morning for a CT scan and completed labs, with an appointment scheduled with the oncology dr for the afternoon. On a light note, we stopped by the jewelry store to discuss getting my ring resized (John guessed I was a size seven on faith and a bit of misdirection from family/friends). Any guesses on my ACTUAL ring size? 5 1/4! Needless to say, we'll have to get it sized down a bit. We came up with a temporary fix for now because I've been losing/gaining weight so quickly with chemo, I didn't want to resize it too soon before we had an idea of the plan moving forward. To be fair, if John had asked me my ring size I wouldn't have known it either, so he didn't do too terrible.

The doctor appointment itself resulted about as I expected. I've had increased pain in my chest, especially the right/center. The cancer spots are "stable" as described by the doctor, but the bone pain is likely more widespread because it's in the bone marrow and is moving all around the other bones in my body like my sternum and ribs.

Labs are stable! We had to change some medication due to beginning chemo again on Monday, so I'm working through my pain with morphine now and it makes me extremely tired and emotional. If I randomly start crying, then laughing because I'm crying, then pass out mid-sentence... blame the drugs. I think I cried over three separate subjects last night in the matter of five minutes, and a missed exit on the interstate almost sent me into hysterics. I'm sure I'm just a joy for my family to be around lately!

As mentioned, chemo starts on Monday and we'll do a full 48 hours of chemo and it's expected that I'll be back in the hospital for another 2 weeks for recovery as my counts bounce around. We'll also start with some genetic testing on Monday to send to Mayo in Rochester to hopefully find a chemo that works better with my specific genes. The test takes a few weeks to process, so hopefully everything will line up appropriately as we are scheduled to go to Rochester around the first week of May. After this next round of chemo, we will do another CT scan and PET scan to see how things are working, but was told yesterday we may never figure out the origin of the cancer.

We'll post more next week when chemo starts up again! Hopefully things are easier with this round than the last one, and if my delirium gets too crazy I pray Jes posts for me again so I'm not going on and on about tuna sandwich smelling MRI machines! Sending love.

Alcester-Hudson Elementary supporting Angie as she starts Round 2 of Chemo. A proud alumnus of A-H, Angie was touched by the outpouring of support from kids she had never met. Angie's nieces, Aleigha and Charley are holding the sign at either end.

CHAPTER 13

Spacesuits

CARINGBRIDGE POST
by Angela Hazel, April 13, 2017

The Hazel's checked back into the Avera hotel on Monday to start Round 2 of chemo! The doc ran one chemo drug on Monday after we were admitted and got all of our preliminary work done, and I had a FULL day of chemo on Tuesday. After a good night's sleep, I woke up Wednesday morning feelin' fine, but things went downhill since. :(We're working through some aches and low appetite mostly. We spoke with palliative care and tried switching things around and scheduling my nausea and pain meds vs. waiting until I was in dire need and having to ask for medication; it has helped a lot! This weekend will be when my numbers hit their lows, so we're planning to just take it easy and one day at a time!

Some other grim news: I have shingles. Evidently, it's pretty common with chemo due to a low immune system and high stress. We caught it really early (a midnight call to the doctor on the weekend, following up the next day with more phone calls and pictures texted to the doctor lead to getting the script filled and started before admission) so it couldn't spread too far and we're already looking to the drying up stage. It does mean that I have to be on airborne precautions and in isolation, so everyone coming in to my room is gowned up from head to toe and masked. It makes me feel a little bit like Tandy and the gang from "Last Man on Earth" when Tandy's brother and Pat show up in their spacesuits (if you don't think understand my reference, go back and watch "Last Man on Earth" from season one and talk to me when you're finished. It's John and my favorite show, you won't regret it! See our Halloween costumes circa 2015!)

Not too much to report on from the hospital bed this week, which is good! Labs are looking normal, and all the problems I was having with my breathing and heart rate last time are resolved. I've found the fewer doctors that visit your room, the better, and I'm usually down to just one or two doctors per day now. Let's rejoice!

I need to take a second to give a huge shout out to my Mom. She has been beyond amazing throughout this entire diagnosis. We've each had our rough moments where we've needed to lean on each other and she has always been my rock. And for her to cuddle up on a less than comfortable fold out chair to sleep every night? Poor lady! She's going to need a massage after this week, that's for sure. I pray for my Mom and Dad every day, but if I could request an extra prayer for them from you all too, I'd greatly appreciate it! This is as much their journey as it is mine.

♡Angie

Carter's Perspective

Avera is home again. Palliative care is back but this time I am more tolerable as it is more about getting to know Angie and keeping her as pain free as possible. They are good people with a job I would never want.

This time around seems a little less frightening as I suppose I'm starting to understand the routine and learning the drugs and what they are for. Angie has once again amazed me with her ability to retain so much information despite the amount of painkillers she is on.

Cassy's Perspective

Round two has begun and we're still trying to decide if it's harder or easier than the first time.

The first round of chemo was such a whirlwind, foreign territory, and unbelievably scary. But the grim reality we were in, didn't seem like reality at all. It was some other girl's life that was crashing in and the Hazel's were just observing. Unfortunate witnesses of a horrific car accident, we wanted desperately to look away but couldn't. We didn't stop to think, we just kept pushing forward trying to get out of this panicking nightmare. We were all trying to be helpful, but nothing was ever enough to make it go away. I think it would have hurt less if this diagnosis had been mine than my baby sister's.

Round two is when reality actually began to sink in and I had to begin to accept that Angie's cancer was not going away. The bruises from the first fight were still fresh from her opponent playing a dirty game. The cuts were deep and yet she went back for more because she fought a good fight, learned a few moves and she had a huge team backing her up. She knew what was coming this time around and that fighting the devil was her only option.

CHAPTER 14

Simple Requests

CARINGBRIDGE POST
by Angela Hazel, April 17, 2017

Happy Easter! Our Easter celebration at the hospital was a bit less than traditional, but we had good company including an aunt, uncle, two grandmas and my Mom and Dad. John and I shared a fair amount of Cadbury mini eggs as well, so we definitely weren't deprived by any means!

A new week brings new discussion with my treatment now that my normal doc is back from his own Easter vacation. We found out the tissue sample from Kansas City was sent to Boston to begin the genomics testing and crossing our fingers there is enough of the sample left without having to do another biopsy (just for ease and time sake). We also nailed down plans to go to Rochester the first week in May to see what they can do for us there, but no word yet on if I'll be admitted or how long treatment would be there. We had a blood transfusion this weekend, so once I got over the initial hee-bee jee-bees of having someone else's blood in my body, we got that started without hiccups. My white cell count has fallen again, as expected, so I'll be admitted until that count recovers at the end of the week provided no sneaky fevers or infections creep up.

After discharge, I am hoping to make it back to Kansas City for a few days at least! John's working on getting me down there so I can cook a meal of my own and have a cup of coffee on my back deck, my two biggest requests after being away from home for the past 6 weeks!

Cinties Perspective

Looking to the future, Angie is hoping to go to Kansas City after this round. I look at this as a double-sided sword. On one side, I want to keep her close by and help her. On the other side, I know John and her need some of their own time and he will take very good care of her as he always has.

John and Angie are very fortunate to have some of their best friends living right there nearby in Kansas City. They were willing to come and help with anything needed and sit with Angie to keep her company when John was gone for work. They have been here every step of the way. Friends like that are hard to find.

Cassys Perspective

Ang was starting to get stir crazy after being cooped up at either the hospital or Mom and Dad's the last six weeks. She wanted to go home, to her own sanctuary. Sleep in her own bed, make her own meals, spend time with her fiancé and friends–normal 26-year-old things. Who could blame her? We were trying not to take it personally but none of us liked the idea of her being so far from us. Especially after how hard it was to get her to come back to South Dakota in the first place. She and her doctors assured us it would be OK, she was in good hands but I'm quite positive it was killing Mom no matter how hard she was trying to convince herself otherwise.

Mayo, on the other hand, I could not wait to send her on the road.

CHAPTER 15

Stress Be Gone!

CARINGBRIDGE POST
by Angela Hazel, April 20, 2017

Sleep is evading me tonight, but I think that may be due to the fact that I'm so excited at the possibility that I may go home tomorrow or Saturday! In a VERY rare situation I may be discharged today, but in order for that to happen, my white cell count would have had to had bottomed out yesterday and I would have to have a very trusting doc! It's been a long 10 days, I can't wait to be discharged soon!

With that said, I had a tough evening/morning of headaches and nausea recently, so it may be best for me to hang tight at the hospital for another day or so (that, and the fact that we finally got Hulu and Netflix set up on the big screen so we can binge watch some new tv). We're thinking the headache was due to switching around some medications, but either way I'm feeling much better now! Everyone, including the docs, nurses, and my family is really impressed with how much better this round went compared to the last. Smooth sailing!

The past week has been incredible with other types of healing as well thanks to my awesome family, friends, and even kind strangers! My aunt was kind enough to give me an amazing foot massage with some essential oils and set up a Singing Bowls session at the hospital. If you are unfamiliar with this alternative medicine technique as I was, YouTube it. It was so interesting and relaxing! I definitely felt like my body relaxed in a way I can't usually achieve during the day, it was so uplifting! We also had visits from our pastor and prayers with family friends, resulting in sharing new books and discussions about reframing the way we talk about God and my diagnosis, which was really eye opening. I feel like this journey is teaching me something every day, and the walk with God is bringing me closer daily as well.

To contribute to other stress relief, we found out the great works from the various benefits going on in my honor. It's so humbling, I can barely find words. I've just bawled from all the support I've gotten... it's been incredibly overwhelming. A beautiful fundraiser at work not only left the hospital system I work for adorned in awesome Team Angie t-shirts, but helped set up my family financially as well. The fundraiser at LaurieBelle's in Tea raised an incredibly generous amount, and I can't even begin to thank Laurie for everything she and her staff did on my behalf to pull it off (I heard the store was PACKED both days and online orders were crazy as well!). And THANK YOU to everyone who came/supported!! Any excuse to shop is a good one in my opinion, but this is so above and beyond my wildest dreams, it's hard to even wrap my head around. Then of course, there is the benefit at Waddy's tonight. I can't believe the generosity of everyone involved...all I can say is what I've said before; thank you and I'm so grateful. The stress of medical bills has been lifted and I thank God for every penny.

Cassy's Perspective

I've always felt that there are many more ways to heal someone than going to the doctor and getting a prescription. It was wonderful to hear Angie was opening up to some alternative methods, it's hard though when you have people coming at you from every direction promising that their way is the best. This is when you pray to God to put you in the right hands at the right moment each day. This certainly seemed to be happening in our situation or we never would have had the support from so many amazing people. Whether it was medically, emotionally, spiritually or financially the love for Angie was coming out of the woodworks.

Cinters Perspective

The support Angie had was overwhelming. The list of fundraisers goes on and on. That was an enormous stress reliever. It wasn't just about the financial fundraisers however, the home cooked meals, the prayer chains, and even the simple checking-in texts and good-will messages gave us the strength to keep pushing forward knowing we were supported by our village. God's grace is good.

CHAPTER 16

Kansas City, Here I Come

CARINGBRIDGE POST
by Angela Hazel, April 22, 2017

For anyone that missed the Facebook/Instagram post, I was discharged on Thursday! We're back at home in Kansas City for a few days before heading up to Rochester, which was my only wish between these next couple rounds of chemo. Thankfully John has been back and forth, and we had friends checking on the house, so there weren't too many surprises (just a bag of overlooked rotten potatoes in the pantry) when we arrived home.

To start from the beginning, John and I hit the road not knowing what to expect but hoping for the best. We knew that my hips would need some help, so we stacked a soft pillow on the seat for me to sit on and that did the trick! I was sure to keep up on my pain meds and before I knew it, we were pulling into my driveway with only a couple aches and pains! The seven-hour drive to Rochester next week should be easy peasy!

The real surprise struck me when we pulled in to our house. Our neighbors in the ol' cul-de-sac had a beautiful "welcome home" sign printed and hung it on the garage doors, as well as my WIC coworkers decorating our lawn with purple flamingos, an awesome sign and the biggest balloons I've ever seen! See the picture! I just cried when we pulled in, what an awesome sight!

Before wrapping up, I want to say a HUGE thank you to everyone that helped out with the Waddy's fundraiser on Thursday night. From the generous, hardworking staff donating their hard-earned tips, to the volunteers that cleaned tables, to those who showed up to eat a delicious meal... I have so much gratitude! This community blows my mind when it comes to helping those in need. Other than the Waddy's fundraiser, I want to say thank you for all the other fundraisers going on recently to help me out as well, such as the cookie dough sales, the homemade body butter and skin care, bracelets/hats/shirts, Lauriebelle's, Easter M&M sales, a lemonade stand, Tastefully Simple, Lipsense, photography packages, The Little Cellar Wine Company, my grandma's quilt...the list goes on and on! How proud I am to know such kind and Godly people!

Angie's welcome home.

John's Perspective

How I processed Angie's sickness was similar to what I try to do with work or my personal life: set some goals. I tried to have Angie view it the same. First goal was to get through that first week. Second goal was to get her in a situation where she could get out of the hospital. We set goals along the way, things we would strive for until she would beat her situation. Things such as getting her back to Kansas City to our house. We accomplished almost all of the goals we set along the way. The one goal we didn't achieve ended up being one that was trumped by a higher power's goal.

On the topic of work, personal life, and balancing Angie's treatment, that was an area that provided some unique challenges but I could only appreciate the support I had there as well. I was able to work remotely as needed, Angie was close to family and friends so I trusted the support system in place when I traveled, and an employer that was more than understanding and supportive from management down to my peers, Angie's was no different throughout. My time and energy would shift and adjust as needed, it was so important not to have any outside stresses. The house back home was being watched by neighbors, it truly allowed us to focus on the task at hand, which was paramount. Not being overly familiar with the medical field going into this and all of us being thrust into it; the various doctor appointments, labs completed, general monitoring of Angie's symptoms, chemo drug names, and the overwhelming amount of medications. Of those medications, which one's can and cannot be cycled together, how often you need to cycle. There are so many things that you need to stay in front of, or you pay a larger consequence if you fail to do so. Through the experience one thing was evident, if we didn't stay ahead of pain management, it would be very impactful as to if it was a good day or not! I'll never forget but before we left for Sioux Falls, a time Angie got out of bed, took two steps, and collapsed strictly from the pain being so overpowering. During the next four months that pain (and drug routine) only became stronger. No worse feeling than knowing there is absolutely nothing you can do to fix a problem staring you right in your face.

A feeling that throughout this process you almost have to accept. There were so many people day in and out who tried everything they knew but could only do so much. Angie was fragile and had to be treated as such while also balancing trying to keep things as normal as possible. Things are tough to see as normal though when at times you can only walk a couple hundred feet before you are exhausted for the day.

CHAPTER 17

Mayo Clinic Visit Update

CARINGBRIDGE POST
by Angela Hazel, May 3, 2017

I have a request of everyone–lay down in your bed tonight and just soak it in. How awesome does it feel to be hugged by a mattress that knows your dips and curves of your body, to wake up with the sun peeking through the blinds, to even smell coffee brewing in the house in the morning, knowing you didn't have to spend $4 at a coffee kiosk in the hospital to get it? I was SO grateful to be able to spend some time in Kansas City this week. What a relief it was to be home! John, Doug, Andrea and Julia were awesome caregivers and made sure I was safe and helped me plan an awesome get together with neighbors and friends! We had an awesome time despite a nasty thunderstorm that rolled in the day prior to our party. Sending out a huge thank you to everyone for coming!

On Sunday we drove to Rochester to be seen by the sarcoma team at the Mayo Clinic. While they are still not 100% sure I even have sarcoma, they will continue to treat it as such and aren't too worried about finding the origin anymore if the chemo is working as is. We won't be doing another scan (pet, MRI, CT, etc.) until after the third round as we already did one after the first round, and routinely they don't do them after each round anyhow. We believe the chemo is working because I honestly feel SO. GOOD. Don't get me wrong, I do still have to take extra medicine for breakthrough pain here and there in addition to feeling very sore and tired quickly, but I definitely feel better than I did before treatment started.

The doc at Mayo didn't have much new news for us. He said that we are already on the right track with the chemo that my doctor in Sioux Falls had me on now, and let us know that we do have other options for chemo after this is done, which is encouraging because my body/organs can only tolerate 4 rounds of this chemo regimen before bad things happen. He suggested we continue to move forward with genomics and basically reassured us that everything being done in Sioux Falls is just as they would be doing up there. More good news; my doc called me today and said that we can hope and assume my body can handle the chemo this time as well as it did last time and we can try to discharge me after 2-3 days rather than staying in the hospital for the 2 weeks like we've done in the past. Can I get a Hallelujah?!!

What an exciting few days we've had! Now off to relax with my family in South Dakota and help my nieces finish their school year. We have declam and track and field this week, and Char and Al need a cheering section for each. Count me in!

Angie cheering on her nieces during their elementary Track and Field events.

Carter's Perspective

Off to the unknown. Rochester, here we come. That experience was crazy. Everything in Rochester works like a well-oiled machine. We were only there for three and a half hours and received good news and bad news.

The good news: the doctors in Sioux Falls are doing everything that they would be doing in Rochester. It was comforting to know we have such good current doctors so close to home.

The bad news: the doctors in Rochester did not have any miracles up their sleeves.

The trip itself was good, as Angie got to play catch-up with a good friend from college. They never get to see each other enough. We also had the opportunity to take the long route home and spent the night at my Dad's. It was good to visit without being in the hospital. We went to my nephew's hockey game and out for supper. As always, Angie handled it all like a trooper and never complained. On the way home, Russ asked Angie if there was anything she wanted to do. She said she wanted to go on vacation with all of us and to go wedding dress shopping. We were determined to fulfill her wishes.

Cassy's Perspective

In my mind, Mayo was where people went to make dreams come true, like Disney World for the sick and injured. It was for those desperate to find a cure for something bigger than most hospital teams could handle. There had to be an answer, a game plan that these doctors would have for Angie. They'd take one look at her and say, "You don't have cancer of an unknown primary...it's not MAYBE sarcoma, you have_____, and we can fix it!"

Unfortunately, that didn't happen, not even close. All morning I waited on pins and needles for texts or phone calls from our parents. I was expecting in depth tests, maybe a hospitalization and hopefully a better-looking diagnosis. But noon arrived, and Mom, Dad, Ang and John had packed up and started home. No better off than she was when she left. Sioux Falls was already doing everything they could, and while that should have made me feel better, it just made me feel worse. It was not enough.

CHAPTER 18

Round Three Kick To The Face–But Still In The Fight!

CARINGBRIDGE POST
by Angela Hazel, May 12, 2017

Round three––what can I say other than ouch? Chemo was not as gentle on me this time as the last. We went into chemo on Monday after a very winded and sleepy weekend, and I definitely wasn't on my A game emotionally. Despite those facts, chemo went off without a hitch and my doctor was able to discharge me on Wednesday rather than spending a week and a half to two weeks in the hospital like normal, with strict instructions to treat myself like the bubble boy for the next week. I'm grateful for the chance to recover at home, but Wednesday night and yesterday were TOUGH. John said I was battling my chemo hangover, and that's about the best way to describe it.

Yesterday we called the doctor because I couldn't get on top of my nausea and just felt...unsettled. Out of my body. Uncomfortable. I didn't spike a fever or show any other signs of infection, so we returned to the Prairie Center as an outpatient for fluids and a shot that prevents my white cell count from bottoming out too much. While there, we ran into our chaplain that has helped us through this process and she brought up the Dutch word of "benout", which perfectly describes my feelings...no real symptoms other than nausea, but just felt lousy, to the point where I was in tears most of the day. She stayed and prayed with my family and a feeling of calm washed over me. I felt stronger and more at peace with God's presence. My Mom prayed for good sleep and that's exactly what I got...over 12 hours of mostly uninterrupted sleep.

Thankfully John came back yesterday as well, and his presence after over a week without him was just what the doctor ordered. We're hoping to make it back down to KC soon, but no visitors until my white cell count bottoms out (and extra Purell for John and I!).

We heard back on some big news this week about the genomics testing. The blood test and tissue test both identified an abnormal mutation in the BRAF gene that is likely the driver of the cancer and there are 5 chemo drugs that can tackle that type of mutation. The tissue found 3 other mutations, only one of which has a chemo drug to fight it, but they said we don't necessarily have to fight each alteration, that maybe fighting BRAF and FANCC will be enough. The drug companies have technically not approved the chemo drugs for sarcoma treatment (one is a melanoma and the other is an ovarian cancer drug) so we have our patient advocate working on getting the insurance company to approve it for treatment or getting the drug company on board for reducing/covering the cost.

They also identified that my tumor mutation burden is considered "intermediate", meaning I could use immunotherapy to fight the cancer too. This would allow my own immune system to learn to fight the cancer. There are two drugs they could use to do this and would add that on to the next round of chemo.

This new info doesn't alter our plan, but rather defines our next step. We will still do one more round of IMAP chemo and then do a scan to see how well things are working. If the IMAP is working and my body can handle it, we could potentially max out the IMAP by doing 5-6 rounds total, then switching to the new regimen. If the cancer is stable or growing, we'll move on to the new chemo.

This journey has been easier than I could have expected most days, but harder than I could have imagined on other days. Every day I thank God for the prayers and love. This week my parents received an awesome gift from God...farmers from all over the area came over to help my Dad disc and plant. What a blessing to have this stress taken off of his shoulders!

Cassy's Perspective

Finally, after 2 months it felt like we were finally getting some answers. It was a relief to know a piece of the puzzle had been found and we had a treatment option for after Angie was done with her next couple rounds of chemo. I, as I'm sure many others were, was worried when we kept hearing she was getting the strongest type of chemotherapy possible for as long as her body could handle it yet we still don't know exactly what she was fighting. What would we do then? Give up? We were all very grateful to have this new spec of light in this deep, dark cave we were trying to escape.

Cinter's Perspective

This round was tough, definitely should have stayed in the hospital longer. With that being said, we ended up going back to the Prairie Center for some fluids and got to see Angie's earth angel, her chaplain. It is always a God Thing with her. It doesn't seem like we hardly ever have to ask to see her, she just always seems to show up when we need her, whether it is at the hospital or at the Prairie Center. When she speaks with Angie, she always knows what to say to calm her.

This round, another large God Thing occurred. All of our neighbors and friends came to help put in the crop and serve dinner and lunch to the workers. Once again, saying thank you never seems like enough. This lifts a tremendous burden off Russ' shoulders as he fights everyday with himself as to how to divide his time between the farm, work, or with Angie. This was so much more than planting a crop, this gave him a piece of peace, one less thing to worry about.

Jenny's Perspective

Our Dad is the kind of guy that carries the weight of the world on his shoulders. A man who raises his hand any time he sees a need. He has been on almost every local committee, every nonprofit/church/township board that needed him. He is a proud member of the volunteer fire department and like so many others has dropped everything he is doing countless times to tend to an emergency or help those in need. He will do anything for anyone and never expects anything in return.

So, when his cousin and neighbors started organizing a day to help him and his brother Mark get the crop in, Dad was at a loss for words. Of course, they would help, my Dad had participated in so many similar events over the years, helping neighbors plant or harvest when they had catastrophes of their own occur. But to be part of the receiving end of that help was unnatural and humbling. There is no way to even put into words how grateful we were.

CHAPTER 19

An Unexpected 4 A.M. ED Visit

CARINGBRIDGE POST
by Angela Hazel, June 4, 2017

As we lace up our gloves for round 4 of chemo, I'd like to reflect back on the last few weeks. My family swears a bit of my hair is growing back, but I don't see it (maybe I'm just impatient). I did take better care of my head the past few weeks and took precautions to prevent a sunburn on my noggin after round one. I got to spend some quality time with friends that traveled from Denver, Scottsdale, and Manhattan, KS during my time at home after my last treatment. It was so much fun! I also got the chance to cook some good meals initially when I arrived home, but that came to a skidding halt when I began to feel nauseous early last week.

John and I had a great time visiting his brother, sister-in-law, nephews and nieces at their lake cabin for 5 days, filled with leisurely boat rides, delicious donuts, and fun family bonding. The campfires felt amazing, but my lungs didn't appreciate the campfire smoke very much and this made it a struggle to breathe. As of the Thursday or Friday before Memorial Day, I felt my health start the slow slide downhill. By Monday, I was having slight bone pain in my shoulders and the inside of my hips, near my lymph nodes. By Tuesday, I was playing phone tag with my oncology doc to see what I could/needed to do to muscle through until my appt on June 5th before I am admitted for chemo. I finished up the week by driving back to SD on Friday with John to meet up with some friends for a poolside birthday party. We had an awesome day, but I may have overestimated my stamina...by 8 pm I was in such intense bone pain in my shoulders and ribs and running so short of breath that I was ready to go to the ED. We held off for a few hours, but by 3:30 am it was undeniable...I couldn't control that type of pain.

We were admitted to the ED and I received IV pain meds and a chest X-ray that determined nothing was broken or fractured (what a relief!!). Since then my pain has been coming in strong waves all day, about bringing me to my knees at points, even with taking morphine around the clock.

We'll know more tomorrow after we follow up with my doctor, and I may have John do our next post if they keep me on the same pain med dosage as before. I can't keep my eyes open long enough to type a single sentence. I know I have a lot of people praying out there for me, and this week more than ever I could use them. Hopefully this pain will pass soon and we can continue on with our treatment plan. Love you all!

♡Angie

Carter's Perspective

Round 4 of chemo was coming, which translates to the week before chemo. We had been noticing that things got tougher for Angie that week before chemo. As I look back at Angie's chemo sessions and the time in between, the number of good days seemed to be getting fewer and fewer. It really made me wonder about her next scan. In the beginning, we asked how we would know if the chemo was working. Her doctor said, the biggest indicator would be how she is feeling.

It was wonderful John and Ang got to go have some normal time at the lake and make some memories. It is never fun to go to ED, but we thank God that the ED doctors and staff are there to help her when she needs them.

Jerry's Perspective

Somewhere between the Mayo trip, Round 4 of chemo, and just generally watching Angie progress as she fought, my prayers started changing. Initially, I prayed the same thing everyone else was, for a miracle. I prayed that God would save my sister. I prayed that He would bring His mighty healing powers and remove the cancer from her body. I prayed every version of *"heal her"* that I knew. I reminded Him that I knew the stories told in His bible, I *knew* He could do it. But I saw her getting worse, instead of better, even though I was praying as hard as I could. Instead of peace, all it left me with was growing anxiety.

So slowly these prayers for a Hail Mary, begging for that mighty miracle from our Lord and Savior transformed. I started adding to my prayers, that He would guide us each day and give us the presence of mind to make the most of whatever time we had left. That He would help me have grace with myself and our family as we navigated all these overwhelming emotions. Most of all I prayed for understanding, that He would help me find a place of peace no matter what the outcome was, that He would help me comprehend the purpose of all of this.

As I saw her slipping, I needed a big picture view. Changing my prayers helped me appreciate every moment I had with her. I realized that whether or not God saved her was *not dependent* on how hard I prayed. The way I reacted to every bump in the road *was*, however. I firmly believe that the prayers of understanding and guidance through the trials helped me see the little things God was doing along the way. The God Things. It opened up my heart to God's will and the way He was using Angie and all of us.

Everyday my heart still hurt, pleading for that miracle, but my soul was beginning to feel peace that no matter what, God was still holding us tight.

◆

Cassy's Perspective

I had a hard time knowing that Jessy felt Angie might not make it. To think life would go on without Angie being here to experience it was still hard for me to think about. I've lost a best friend before, I know the steps of grief and that eventually the sorrow lets up enough to let you breathe again, but I also know how hard it is for those that need to continue each day, to put one foot in front of the other when each step feels harder than the last.

Losing my sister though would be an entirely different experience. We had an amazing bond and shared each childhood memory together. To be at a place of acceptance, knowing we likely wouldn't be with Angie for many years to come, was nearly impossible. I wasn't sure I'd ever be able to comprehend the purpose of this all as Jessy was trying so hard to do.

CHAPTER 20

Summary Vacationing At Avera

CARINGBRIDGE POST
by Angela Hazel, June 9, 2017

After camping out at Avera National Park all week (truthfully, I've been seeing everyone else's pictures of hiking and vacation trips and I'm so jealous! I can't wait until I'm feeling well enough to get back into nature), I'm ready to hit the road again.

We had a relatively smooth ride during this hospitalization after handling the emergency room visit this weekend. Chemo itself went well, but the side effects this time were nasty, causing more nausea than I've ever had and a scary moment where I almost passed out in the shower. Thankfully John was within earshot, so he helped me to the seat and called for the nurse right away. I'm so proud of him, he knew just what to do in the midst of the situation. My blood pressure was low, but I was fine after a few minutes because of the quick reactions everyone had. I knew I was okay when silly me kept thinking about all the people who saw me in my naked glory, and how embarrassing that was!

We added more pain patches to my shoulders, where the pain is most significant. Hopefully this will be enough as we have big plans for the next couple weeks with friends visiting and quality family time planned. We'll play it by ear until our scan in 3 weeks and determine what the next step is after that!

Carter's Perspective

At Angie's request, we went wedding dress shopping the day after she was discharged from Round 4. Angie had made the appointment at the dress shop and my girls, Grandmama and John's Mom and sister all went.

Jessy and Cassy went to the shop early and explained exactly what was going on, and that Angie probably wouldn't have enough energy to last much more than a half hour. The girls picked out dresses based on styles Angie shared from Pinterest, so energy wouldn't be wasted on dresses she didn't like.

John's sister and Mom brought alcohol-free champagne and "Say Yes to the Dress" signs. Cassy helped Angie change into every dress, so they wouldn't be as heavy when taking them on and off. We had a great time gushing over the dresses, commenting on how beautiful Angie looked in each.

Then, a few dresses in, Angie found the *Yes Dress* and despite the pain patches on her shoulders and a lopsided messy wig (she was more beautiful bald) Angie was the most fabulous looking bride I have ever seen. She was breathtaking and just glowed.

I offered to buy the dress right there on the spot, but Angie said no, not yet, reasoning, she still wanted to shop with her friends, too, and not be done in the first store she went to.

Angie lasted almost an hour and a half that day, much beyond anyone's expectations. We took lots of pictures and wrote the info down so when she was ready, we could come back for the dress.

Cassy's Perspective

Helping Angie shop for a wedding dress was something I had always looked forward to.

Going back a few years to when it was my turn to wedding dress shop, I remember Angie being just as excited as well. That day for whatever reason Angie was running late and Jessy couldn't be there. Mom and I started browsing a couple stores thinking this would be a several outing experience as that's how it went for Jessy when she was gown shopping and just based on how horrendously indecisive I am. But not more than 6 or 7 dresses into the day, I had found "the dress." When Angie finally arrived, fashionably late, she was so annoyed that I had found the dress without her. She kept questioning me, "Are you sure, are you sure this is the one?" Not because she didn't like it but because the experience she had been waiting for so long was over.

Now, I could completely relate. When I pictured her in her wedding dress I never envisioned she wouldn't have her hair or would have to wear pain patches, the sympathy stares from other shoppers or subpar customer service just because the saleswoman knew we were just browsing. But in spite of all that, she was still beautiful. Absolutely jaw-dropping beautiful. She was glowing from within and you could tell she was having an amazing time.

Angie took what she knew was going to be an emotionally difficult day and turned it into something unforgettable. That was Ang in a nutshell, so positive and uplifting. She knew it was hard not just on her but on all of us, questioning if she'd ever get to walk down that aisle and living her happily ever after.

A toast to Angie and a great day at the bridal store.

CHAPTER 21

Feeling The Love

CARINGBRIDGE POST
by Angela Hazel, June 13, 2017

I need to take a moment to give thanks and praise for everyone that has been by my side during the past few months! Sometimes the feelings are overwhelming, but the love that pours out from people in the community and my friends and family is hard to comprehend! I could not do this without my family's positive thinking and prayers, nor could I do this without the faith community in the area thinking of my family daily. John has been so patient and takes the ups and downs as they come much better than I could have guessed or assumed. My work family has poured out their support and kept tabs on me, and my soon to be in-laws stepped up immediately to help us through. I've had days where I've felt like giving up, but I can't. I owe too much to God for giving me this beautiful life and giving me another day. I won't take it for granted!

♡Angie

Jerry's Perspective

For years, Ang had been trying to prove to the world that she could tackle it head-on, on her own. Maybe this was more evident from the viewpoint of being her big sister. So many phone calls and visits where she was going above and beyond to show her family, or maybe just me, that she was responsible, an adult, and capable of declaring her own path.

While all of this was true, it all came around full circle the sicker she became. Trivial things she used to easily do she was now needing help with. Chemo brain was taking over, and no matter how hard she tried to stay organized and mindful, she became forgetful and distracted. I kept reminding her it was ok. Everyone needs someone. Humans were not designed to live a life of solitary. She needed us as much as we needed her. A shoulder to cry on, someone quiet to sit in the dark with a much-needed laugh, an extra set of ears to absorb tough news, and an extra mind to contemplate difficult decisions.

Sometimes the lines were fuzzy. She was the patient, but we were all mourning the loss of her before she was even gone, all of us trying to soak up every last good moment with her, which sometimes lead to her comforting us instead of us comforting her. At times it was overwhelming for her, even during the happy moments. Being surrounded by people you love sounds like a wonderful gift and for the most part it is, but she needed her space too.

Like anyone up against death, she was starting to sort out her life, mindfully taking inventory of everything she had done. Like a kid at Christmas time determining if they were "good" enough for Santa to stop, she was considering all her wrongdoings and wondering if she would make it through the gates of Heaven when it was her time. It was heartbreaking seeing her analyze herself with such scrutiny, knowing that her missteps were minor and that she was fully forgiven by her Lord and Savior.

Ang became withdrawn in many situations, present but quietly absorbing the moment, not often commenting or contributing to the conversation. Looking in her eyes it was like she was taking a mental picture or video, like she was memorizing every detail. Filling her mind with good memories to last a lifetime until we would see her again.

Shortly after Ang's first round of chemo, our family started discussing going a family vacation when Ang was strong enough. Multiple destinations were thrown out, all of us asking Ang where she would like to go. We played around with Lake Tahoe, a place Ang had always wanted to see. But quickly it became clear that time no longer passed in days or weeks, instead it was measured in chemo intervals; the time frame of when she would be hospitalized for treatment and the time frame needed to recover. It was clear that there was a short window each month that she would be up to doing any type of trip, and as her cancer progressed, it was clear that the trip should be nearby. We decided to go to Branson, MO, a relatively short car ride from John and Ang's place in Kansas City.

Angie and Mom found a couple cabins to rent at a resort right outside of Branson. The resort had plenty of kid friendly activities and the cabins provided us a place to relax and cook without getting into crowds, and Angie her own space to go lie down whenever she needed.

John, Angie, and Kona stayed in a cabin with Kyle and I and our kids and Mom and Dad, Cassy and Zack and their boys took the other cabin. My kids were SO EXCITED to bunk in the same cabin as Ang and John. They were mindful of the rest and space Ang needed but could barely contain their excitement for several days' worth of sleepovers.

Every day I was amazed by Ang. The way she got up in the morning with no complaints even though you could see on her face it took a lot of effort to get everything moving. The way she quietly took more pain meds and adjusted her pain patches as the day went on, so she could continue to participate, never wanting to be left out. In every action, I could see she was doing everything she could to be present in the moment, to make the most of the trip, to make memories for her nieces and nephews…for all of us.

We had no schedule while there, just doing whatever we felt up to each day. One afternoon, our kids wanted to go to a Bigfoot-themed golf course and outdoor maze. Angie, John and Mom ended up along with Kyle and I as the rest of the crew went to the fish hatchery. We arrived at this outdoor maze and it is well over 90 degrees out. We all decided to give it a try, Ang included.

We no more than walked in and see there is an option to crawl into a tunnel. In our "why not?" spirit of the day, we all decide to follow the kids into this tunnel, thinking it just comes out on the other side of the partition. It wasn't until all four of us adults were crawling around on our hands and knees underground in what can only be described as a "clean sewer system" where we realized we might have made the wrong choice.

The underground portion of the maze was metal tunnels, leading in every direction, with a grate ever so often leading to fresh air above. There was no clear path to get out and there we were crawling around with a cancer patient, a grandma with two replaced knees and three kids on a very hot, humid summer day.

Kyle, John and I nervously gave each other "the look" as we quickly tried to find the nearest exit. Leading ahead, Kyle, John and the kids found daylight with Angie, Mom and I following. Ang crawled out ahead of me. As I crawled out of the tunnel, I saw her drenched in sweat, sitting on a wood platform, leaned up against a pole chugging water and fanning herself with her hand. Mom was following behind me and emerged from the tunnel dripping sweat. I look up and saw the kids reached the top of this platform and were yelling back down that it was a dead end. Mom, who is always notoriously overheated, looked at Angie with sweat running down her face and said "What's wrong with you? Why are you so hot?" Ang whipped off her wig and said, "I have this damn cat on my head, that's why!" We all lost it, laughing so hard. She threw the wig at Kyle and said "Here, shove this in your cargo pocket."

When we all regained our composure, we realized there was no way out of this but back into the tunnel. I was ready to call the employees over, to inform them they needed to break out the chain cutters and make a hole through the fencing to let her out but Ang was adamant she was ok. Into the tunnel we all went again, with John and Kyle scoping out the best route to a clear exit. Finally, the exit was found, and it was an uphill grade on the slippery metal tunnel. John made it out first and tried to help Ang out. She was too far away so he put his leg back into the tunnel, so she could grab on and pulled her out. Our laughter was a combination of the hilarity of the slipperiness of the tunnel and nervousness of the potential severity of the situation, the real possibility of Ang overheating and hurting herself. Finally, her bald head popped out of the tunnel, shirt drenched in sweat and somewhat of a smile still on her face.

Mom was a different story. Kyle jokingly offered to push her out from behind, but she was adamant that was NOT going to happen and made him go ahead of her. She slipped every time she tried to climb the slope, laughing so hard she couldn't gain her bearings and cussing us out for laughing so hard right along with her (or maybe at her). Finally, she ditched her shoes, got some traction with her sweaty toes and climbed the slope with a little pull from Kyle, who still had the "damn cat" in his pocket.

Laughter really is the best medicine.

That weekend we also had a fantastic day driving golf carts through the forest on a paved path, the closest thing that Angie had come to being in nature in months and she was so happy. The path took us through caves, over bridges and next to streams, breathing in the fresh air. Being in the outdoors was one of the things Angie missed most when she was hospitalized.

The rest of the trip was filled with family dinners, swimming, ice cream trips, and just lounging around talking and laughing. We all felt so grateful to have that time together as a family, making memories.

Angie, Anita, Aleigha, Charley and Haizen in Branson.

CHAPTER 22

Progress

CARINGBRIDGE POST
by Angela Hazel, July 3, 2017

First, an apology. I am working to grow closer to family, friends, John and God at this time, meaning I'm spending less time on social media and following my heart to bring me where I need to be in my personal relationships. I love to keep everyone updated on my status, and text messages are wonderful, but I'm trying to live more mindfully and peacefully, meaning I'm spending less time online. I apologize if I haven't responded to messages in a very timely manner, but please know I appreciate every kind word passed on to me. They keep me going day to day!

As an explanation, our doctor's visit resulted in less than desirable news that hit the family hard. While the cancer in the lymph nodes seemed to have stabilized or possibly even improved, the cancer has gotten worse in my bones and in my lungs. The cancer has also spread to my liver. The plan moving forward is that we will move to the genomics chemo and we started immunotherapy today. The good news is that it should have a lot fewer side effects than the IMAP chemo that I was previously on. The bad news is I have been in more pain in the past week than I have in 4 months. We have adjusted pain medications as well as we can for now and will begin taking measurements for radiation next week to help control my pain.

Cancer is tough in general. You wonder if every ache and pain has to do with the cancer itself, or if it was just a simple twinge of day to day living. The only thing that keeps me going is the idea that I can't live my life in fear of the cancer, but rather embrace it as a part of me right now and live my life in spite of the cancer. I need to show the cancer who is boss by not succumbing to the pain and to the fear.

Some wonderful news, as many of you have already seen...John got the most beautiful tribute tattoo for me. I knew for quite some time that he was looking to get a tattoo, but he kept some secrets "up his sleeve" about it if you will. I hope everyone can see it on Facebook, but basically in summary it is a sun with rays of light shining through the clouds, with the face of the sun replaced with a clock symbolically turned to my birthday and our engagement date (04.05). The symbol of peace, a dove, is flying through the rays of light and the backside has our mantra "Faith Over Fear" in a beautiful script. The moment I saw it, I began to cry. Not only is it the most beautiful tattoo I have ever seen, but it was inked on the most beautiful man I've ever seen as well. He is constantly surprising me with how much he loves me, and I feel so unworthy of his unconditional love. As I write this, tears are streaming down my face. I love that man more than I could ever type into words.

♡Angie

 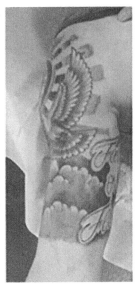 

John's tattoo

Jerry's Perspective

June 30. For years, I have not been able to sleep on June 30. As a kid, it was because it was the night before my birthday, and I eagerly anticipated my birthday every year. As an adult, it became a night where I was restless, thinking about what the last year brought and what another year older would mean. The previous year, it was because we had held my Grandpa Ray's prayer service on the evening of June 30 and I was to give his eulogy at his funeral the next day. But this year, my loss of sleep was because June 30, 2017 was the worst day I have ever had.

The day started out with a lot of nerves for Angie and her appointment. We all anticipated her treatment was not providing the miracle we hoped and prayed for. She was in too much pain, her breathing too hard, for the chemo to be working well. But still, we each started our day with quiet prayers that we were wrong.

The work day began for Cassy and I with unsettling news of big change, creating many unknowns for us both as we work at the same place. Unwelcome change at work as everything in our personal lives already had too many variables. It is hard to gain your bearings when everything is moving at once.

The plan was to have a birthday supper with the whole family at Mom's house that evening to celebrate both mine and John's birthdays the next day. Mom called that afternoon with a change in plans. "Find a place for the kids, we need an adult's only conversation." This wasn't good.

Cassy and Zack, Kyle, and I all walked into Mom's house about the same time. Mom, Dad, Angie, John, Grandmama and Uncle Mark were already there. We made small talk for a few minutes before we all gathered around Angie in the living room.

With tears streaming down her face, she proceeded to tell us that her appointment did not go well. The cancer was spreading, despite the IMAP chemo. This strongest chemo regimen held back the cancer for a while, it bought her some time, but it would not be her miracle. They would try a different chemo and immunotherapy, but neither were expected to work as well as the IMAP did initially. In that conversation, Angie told us that she was dying.

There is nothing more heartbreaking than a room of adults crying. To hear your baby sister say the words out loud. We all knew, but to listen to the words come out of Angie... the hope was gone.

To hear your parents, grandma and uncle sobbing over the news that they will lose the little girl they all worked so hard to raise. To see your husband crying, because he will lose the girl he loved like his own sister from the moment he became part of the family; the girl he so fiercely tried to protect like any big brother would. To see your sister, the one who does not have cancer, broken because no matter what, one sister will never fill the place of two. To see Ang, crying so hard because the life she loves and has fought so hard for is slipping through her fingers.

When it rains it pours.

Sister's Perspective

I can't say I was shocked at the news we received, but I certainly was heartbroken. Our chances of a miracle were getting smaller and smaller, but I continued to hold on to that tiny sliver of hope while cherishing every moment. My goal, personally, was to not have any regrets. To soak up Angie's spirit as much as possible. I prayed for peace continuously.

The day Angie told everyone the chemo was no longer working, everyone was crying. I wanted to go hug them all to help them through this, but I felt that if I even moved I would shatter into a million pieces, never to be the same again. For the rest of our lives, time would be measured before or after Angie's cancer.

Cassy's Perspective

Never in my life have I ever had as big of a wakeup call back to reality as I did on June 30th.

Since March, Angie's cancer had always been at the front of my mind but hearing her say that her cancer was spreading was like a smack in the face. Being beaten within an inch of my life would have hurt less than to hear my sister tell us she was not winning but, in fact, dying. The pit in my stomach grew to the size of a watermelon and I thought I was going to be sick.

Hundreds of people get horrible diagnoses every day and recover. Why couldn't that be her fate? Now what, we have a couple weeks, a few days? This could not be happening.

I looked at my parents and they had never looked so little, like the weight of her news was physically crushing them into the couch. I don't know if being the unfailing positive one this time was a blessing, I was so blindsided, like someone snuck up behind me and hit me in the back of my head with a 2x4. Looking around it was like everyone else knew it was coming but it didn't matter because we all had the same look in our eyes–heartbreak.

To put it lightly, Jessy's 32nd birthday sucked and that's saying a lot considering what she went through on her 31st. But a couple days later, after we had all had a chance to absorb the news somewhat, Angie decided she wanted to take Dad's pontoon out on the lake for a spin. Ang, our parents, Grandmama, Uncle Mark, my boys and myself went to the closest lake and escaped reality for a few hours. We just soaked in the sun and each other. That day was my last "real" moment with Angie. Just a few days later, she was entering hospice.

Center's Perspective

A couple nights later, Angie was really tired, and John was laying down by her. I told her good night and that I loved her. I went downstairs to watch some TV and sleep so I didn't wake Russ up a hundred times during the night getting out of bed, restless and unable to sleep.

Since the beginning, the routine had always been if she needed me she would text me, as it was hard for her to call out loud enough for me to hear. Well, this night, Angie comes downstairs and says, "Mom, I need you." I asked her why she didn't text, but she was already on her way back upstairs. I followed, and John explained Angie was having a hard time breathing and her anxiety was getting the best of her. We worked to slow down her breathing and settle her down. We asked her what she wanted us to do. "Call 911," she said.

"You want us to call the ambulance?"

"Yes," she replied. I called the ambulance. They dispatched the closest unit, the volunteer ambulance from Hudson. Then we remembered the bridge between our house and town was under construction. Russ called back and told them to dispatch another neighboring town and we would meet them at the highway corner.

We proceeded to get Angie into the vehicle. While we would've liked to scoop her up and carry her to the car, her bone pain was too severe to be able to do this so instead we took her hands and slowly trekked to the car stopping every couple of steps to catch her breath. We met the ambulance a few miles away, and I rode in it with her. Her oxygen level read normal but there was nothing normal about her breathing. I just laid my head by her praying and softly trying to calm her.

That was the last time she was home. In reflection, it was better not knowing it would be the last time.

Jenny's Perspective

Angie's lungs were filling up, making breathing difficult and she was back on oxygen. She described the night with the ambulance as the most terrifying experience she has ever went through.

During that hospital stay, a lot of real conversations occurred. The team that has cared for Angie since the beginning gathered with her and went through her options. It was made clear that her breathing episode that caused the middle of the night ambulance ride was not a one-time event. It was due to her lungs filling with cancer and would likely continue to occur as the cancer progressed. The only thing that could be done was to manage it with medications and try to minimize the anxiety and fear that came with it.

The palliative care team that was despised back in March when they were first introduced to our family came actively back into the picture, now seen in a different light. Angie had developed a good relationship with the palliative care doctor and trusted her to guide her to the right decisions. The terrifying conversations that they tried to have in March, now aren't so scary. It was evident they were real decisions that could not be put off any longer.

Angie was asked about what was acceptable to her to endure and what she considered absolutely unacceptable. She stated that she could handle the pain but could not tolerate the feeling of being unable to breathe, like she did the night she was rushed to the hospital. Options were discussed as to where she wanted to spend her final days. Every possible detail was worked out with the team. It reminded me of when a woman is pregnant, and they are asked about their birth plan. Except this was a death plan and it was unreal to think that we were at that point.

One morning, a couple days after Angie's ambulance ride, we get a call from Mom. We needed to meet that afternoon with Angie's care team regarding some important decisions Angie had made.

From the moment Cassy and I entered Angie's room, I was just flooded with a feeling of contentment. Angie almost looked happy. Relaxed. More comfortable than I have seen her in awhile. She proceeded to tell us that after many conversations and considering all of the options, she made the decision to move to the hospice house for her final days. She would be going as soon as a room was available, and she had enough energy for the move.

I was taken aback. I never expected that she would choose to spend her final days any place except home, at the farm. I never expected that she wouldn't want to go back there one more time, knowing it would be her last. But she looked so calm. She clearly made the decision with peace in her heart and a gentle push from God.

Cinter's Perspective

As we met with the palliative care team, I quietly sat there and listened, watching Angie, making sure that she was getting heard and making sure she wasn't feeling rushed about her decisions. We asked all kinds of questions but ultimately when Angie was comfortable, so was I.

This hospital stay, Angie was on the pulmonary floor where everyone was nice, but it certainly wasn't like oncology where everyone knew her name. With the pulmonary floor came a different doctor. Angie requested to see her oncologist one more time to thank him for everything he had done. He stopped in the following day, always so professional. Angie gave him a hug and her thanks.

It wasn't until later that we found out how much Angie impacted him and his staff. We found out that Angie's earth angel, Reverend L., was asked to meet with Angie's oncology team the day she went to hospice to help them process as they all were having a really hard time. Further proof of how Angie touched so many lives, as they deal with cancer patients every day.

CHAPTER 23

Prayers For Peace

CARINGBRIDGE POST
by Jessy Paulson, July 7, 2017

With a peaceful heart, Angie decided to move to Hospice. We ask for continued prayers for God's calming hand. Prayers to keep away anxiety and fear, prayers for strength and courage and prayers for all of her family, friends and the hospice staff to provide her the support she needs.

The love you all are sending throughout this journey is felt very strongly.

Jessy's perspective

Walking into the hospice house, we immediately felt at home. The place was welcoming, serene, and calm, completely unlike the sterile hospital or musty nursing home settings I was expecting.

Angie was transported by ambulance and situated into her new room that had bright windows and a small living room just off of Angie's room for family to spend time in. Visitors were welcomed into the facility with warm cookies and gentle smiles from volunteers.

One of the first people we saw that day are friends of the family, husband and wife volunteers at the hospice house. She was the school nurse when we were kids and had the experience of calling Dad to pick up Angie the day she broke her arm on the playground in kindergarten. "Dad drove as fast as a fire truck that day!" Angie remembered. Seeing familiar faces, caused Cassy to break down immediately. It was a God Thing. Once again, unbelievable how God placed the right people in our path at the right time.

Within a day or two, the hospice house was filled with family and friends of Angie's. Grandparents, nearby family, and friends from across the nation all joined together to see Ang one more time, to be with John and our family, and to just find comfort in each other during a time that did not make sense to any of us.

As we comforted each other we developed the most unlikely relationships and connections. John's family, Angie and John's friends, and our family, all united together, taking turns being the shoulder to cry on between wiping our own tears. Angie's circumstances inevitably rekindled heartbreak from earlier events in everyone's lives. All our previous experiences coloring our current perspective and lending new insight and faith to each other.

Grandmama sticks out to me most at that time. Looking into her eyes you could see her reliving so many hard moments. Reliving the days she faced the previous summer, sitting with my Grandpa while he was on hospice. Reliving the months she cared for her own mother as she fought cancer until the very end. Reliving the pain and heartbreak, decades old, sitting with her own sister during her final days battling leukemia. Grandmama had three young boys at home during that time and was a busy, young farmer's wife. There was no time to process what had occurred, no time to grieve.

Throughout Angie's battle, I felt that no one else understood me the way that my Grandmama did. She had been in my shoes, she had walked down this path. She knew how difficult it was to balance being a Mom, being a wife, and keeping up with work, when all you wanted was for time to stop so you could just be a sister. I could see all this resurface with my grandma, as she was grieving the soon loss of her granddaughter, she was also grieving the past loss of her sister.

One day, Grandmama shared with me that Christmas Eve would

mark forty-five years since her sister had passed. Thinking about it later, I just completely broke down. I cannot fathom living without Angie for forty-five years, a lifetime without my sister.

The hours turned into days. Time was spent quietly telling stories, watching home videos, reminiscing, and feeding Angie her favorite childhood treat, frozen orange pushups, the only thing that could combat the taste of the liquid morphine that lingered in her mouth. Visitors faded in and out of the room as Ang faded in and out of consciousness, always unexpectedly adding to the conversation, often with her feisty sense of humor.

As she progressed, our quiet times of comfort with her were often overtaken by periods of fear and anxiety. When she was able to regain her composure again, she often shouted out, "Go away Devil! You are trying to steal my peace! I am not letting you steal my peace."

When she was unable to fight him off on her own, we all grasped at straws, doing anything to keep her calm, to help her through the moment. Reading scripture, holding her hand, singing songs, chanting mantras, playing music, praying out loud with her, anything to distract her for a moment so she could regain whatever control she had left. Sometimes her episodes were prompted by severe pain that busted through all her medications. Sometimes shortness of breath was the culprit, initiating a full-on anxiety attack. And sometimes it was the sheer weight of processing her life.

One afternoon, I walked into her bedroom. She was sorting through her wallet, which she had asked for just prior to me entering. She had maybe a dozen dollar bills laying in a muddled pile on her lap, unsuccessfully trying to count them. I could see her getting ancy and worked up. I laid my hand on hers and said "Ang, what do you need? Do you want me to count this for you? What are you trying to do?"

She looked up at me, shaking her head, "I don't know. I don't know. I don't know how to do this...I don't know how to die." And we both just cried, because it wasn't about the wallet or the crumpled-up dollar bills. Her body was failing her, she was in so much pain and so ready to go to be free from it, but her mind was still trying to find and finish her unfinished business. She didn't even know what it was that she needed to do because she was only 26 and everything was still unfinished business.

As I regained my composure, I went into the same script we had been using for days to calm her down. "Ang, it's ok. God is with you. You are surrounded by everyone who loves you, we are here for you. You have more family and friends here than anyone, just hanging out in the front family room...."

"Wait. What?" She stopped me mid-sentence. I repeated what I said and reiterated who was in the family room; family and friends from all over the country, all of whom had stopped into her room for a brief moment in the preceding days to send their love. But in the moment, she didn't remember all of that. "What are they doing out there? Why aren't they in here?! Bring them in here! All of them!"

So we recruited all of her visitors in, and her room quickly filled up with close to twenty people within a matter of minutes. And there is Ang again. Suddenly snapped back to herself, welcoming people as they walked in the door.

"You're here! You came all the way from Denver!?!"

"Wow, I can't believe you all are here."

"Kari! You cut your hair! It looks great!"

Within minutes, Ang had the whole room belly-laughing, tears rolling down all of our faces as she told stories and jokes and we saw *her* again. It was so beautiful and so real, and just as quickly as it started, it was over as she ran out of energy and drifted off again.

FAITH OVER FEAR

As posted on Facebook:

Jessy Paulson   •••
July 13, 2017 · 🌐 ▾

I have learned so much from my baby sister throughout this journey. The last
few days she has taught me even more. So often we think that this phase is
about saying goodbye and that's it. But the last few days have shown me
otherwise. It's about helping the one who is dying to grieve the loss of their life,
to grasp the purpose of their life, to be ready to leap into the unknown and trust
God has control. Sometimes this means saying goodbye over and over,
sometimes this means just sitting in the dark quiet night and holding a hand,
sometimes it means sitting in a lobby for days on end doing dozens of puzzles
just so you are there. And every once in a while there is a tremendous
breakthrough like last night where we are reminded she is not done with us yet.
There is so much more to this than just saying goodbye, this is walking her
home. 💜
Faith over Fear Angie Hazel

The days turned into a week, but time stood still every time I walked
into the Hospice House. When I wasn't there, I was still expected
to carry on with my life, take care of my job, my kids, my house.
Yes, we had so much help which I was so grateful for, but I wanted
nothing more than to just stay there with Ang always. To just once
again forget about the rest of the world and only be her sister.

When Ang was calm, we sometimes talked about what Heaven
would be like. How happy she would be to see Grandpa again,
and to talk with him, as he had been non-verbal for months prior
to passing. Joking about what our die-hard Democratic grandpa
would say about the state of the country and election of Trump as
President. We talked about our three siblings that we never met,
miscarriages between me and Cassy and Ang. We wondered if they
were boys or girls. I hoped that there was at least one big sister up
there, ready to welcome her home. Ang promised that she would
save a room in Heaven for me, right next to hers.

One particularly hard day, Ang was in an insurmountable amount
of pain, struggling to breathe, unable to shake the devil fighting
her with every ounce of her being. She begged for relief from the

nurses, who were already pushing everything they possibly could through her. She reminded us all that she was not supposed to feel this way, that this was the thing that was unacceptable to her, that she didn't want to suffocate. She cried out to God that she was ready to go, she begged him to take her. It wasn't the first time, but every time we saw her in this state it became harder. We said every calming thing we could think of, we prayed with her. We asked her what she wanted us to do.

"Pray that God will take me. Pray that this is over."

So we did. We prayed that God would end her suffering now. We prayed that he would take her up to Heaven. We prayed that she would die. Such a stark contrast to the prayers we had been saying daily for the last four months.

And there right in the middle of the room, cradling Ang's hand in her own, was our Mom. Praying harder than any of us. Praying that God would take her baby.

Again, my mind flashed back to Conrad in the hospital so close to death. My heart shattered thinking of the pain my mother was going through. I had spent days praying so hard for God to let my little boy survive, because I could not fathom how I would possibly survive without him. My Mom was so selfless; also knowing that she would struggle to survive without Angie yet no longer praying for a miracle, just praying for peace for her baby. In that moment, I realized the degree of my Mom's faith in God and the sacrifice she was making watching Angie go home to Jesus.

Despite all the prayers, begging, and tears, it wasn't yet her time. She was not called home in that moment or that day. The battle for her peace relentlessly continued on.

From the very beginning when Angie was diagnosed, I deeply felt that she was being lead toward her purpose in life. That something big would come from this. And now it was evident, it wouldn't be a miracle. She wasn't going to become the keynote speaker inspiring others from a podium at national events. She would've been amazing at that. She was instead carrying her story through her people, those that knew her well and even those that knew her as an acquaintance. Throughout her battle as her story was spread, she was bringing others to God; she was sparking faith. Her people vowed to continue to share her life and her story.

She seemed to be the ultimate servant, yet she was continuing to suffer. She was begging for Jesus to save her and He was nowhere to be found. She was banging on Heaven's gates and no one was answering. She was yelling at the top of her lungs "My God, why have you forsaken me?"

None of it made sense. She had been put through hell already, so much stripped from her, why was dying so hard, too?

Going home that night, I prayed while driving like I often did when I was alone.

God, why is this happening? We understand you need Angie, we understand she is fulfilling a greater purpose for you than we can ever imagine, but why the #^@% does it have to be so #^@$!#% hard?

And I stopped as I heard the words out of my mouth. I was using *this* language directly to God. *What was I thinking?* And that's when I decided to screw it. God already knows my every thought, action and prayer. He hears every cry in every language under the sun. If that was the only word I could come up with at the time, He understood. He *knew* it was #^@%#$ up. In that moment, I changed the way I pray. I don't hold back, I don't search for the right words, I say exactly what is on my mind.

When you are so mighty and powerful, how can you let this happen? No mother should ever have to pray for God to take her baby. Ang has given up everything, she has followed you in every way and here she is begging to die, and you are continuing to make her suffer. Why?!?

And in that conversation with God, He gently focused me back in on the purpose of this all. He reminded me he did not inflict this on Ang, the devil did and the devil was trying to steal her peace, even in her final days, just as Ang had been saying. God reminded me He did not leave her, He did not forsake her, or any of us. He was leading us through the storm. He was working to turn around the pain and use it for a great purpose, we just had to continue to have faith. God reminded me that the devil was fighting Him for *my* peace too. Do not let the devil steal your peace.

Cinters Perspective

In the four months since Angie was diagnosed, she managed to maintain her genuine kindness and gratefulness, always flashing her beautiful smile in appreciation. She had a way of keeping us all in check with our own emotions. Since she was able to handle it all gracefully, we could try too. What struck me most is that Angie was inadvertently able to accomplish things my family couldn't do in 51 years. My parents divorced when I was two and each remarried when I was a kid. Over the years, every baptism, confirmation, graduation or any other gathering was always incredibly stressful and awkward because my parents' families would not talk to each other or my foster family. I never felt I could give attention to everyone at these events. During Angie's ordeal with cancer, all my family was around consistently supporting us. Everyone sat in the same area, waited for the same updates, and talked to each other not just about Angie but actually visited. Their love for their granddaughter brought them together peacefully, something I had hoped for, for years.

Angie showed her humor even in hospice. One of the last times Reverend L. visited, she asked Angie if we could pray, as she often did. Angie said, "Yes, of course." Reverend L. said, "Angie it is OK if you fall asleep during, like last time." Reverend L. prayed and when it was over we all opened our eyes and Reverend L. said, "Angie, you didn't fall asleep this time." Angie replied, "You weren't as boring this time." We all had a good laugh. Angie never lost her sense of humor.

Another moment that made us smile was the day Russ went to the pop vending machine at the hospice house. This was during the time frame where Coke was doing their Share a Coke promo where they put people's names on a can or bottle of coke. Russ put in the money and the machine dispensed the next coke, "Angela". Just a little thing. Some may call it a coincidence, but we called it a God Thing. God was letting us know he had everything under control.

God continually brought the people we needed to us. Angie had a close friend who called and texted often only to find out Angie was sleeping again. She decided to send Angie a letter and requested I read it to her. As I did, Angie smiled reminiscing on all their beautiful memories together. A perfect example of the power of words.

God sent us nurses we knew before the hospice house to be part of Angie's care. Nurses who we knew personally and had been down a similar path themselves. They knew there was nothing to say to make it better, but just to be there when we needed them. For this I thanked God.

During those last few days, when Angie was in so much pain and unable to feel comfortable with her breathing, she asked God to take her. She asked us all to pray that it would be over. While all of us prayed and cried over her, I finally prayed, "Thy will be done." I knew if there was no way we were going to get our miracle for her, then I wanted her to go live with Jesus, where she would no longer have any pain. While it would shatter our hearts, she wouldn't be suffering any longer. "Thy will be done, Thy will be done."

Jerry's Perspective

What started out as calming promise when entering the hospice house, soon snapped back to the reality of Angie's very painful cancer. The hospice staff was amazingly attentive; however, Angie began to have more episodes where she struggled to breathe despite the staff's best efforts and best medications. Her anxiety would kick in and she would go into full out panic attacks, trying to catch her breath that just wasn't there as her lungs were filling with cancer. *Feeling* unable to breathe was the one thing that was unacceptable to Ang. She chose the hospice house for her final days specifically, so she wouldn't have to feel like this. And yet she was struggling. And she was panicking. And we all were failing her.

About ten days into hospice care, on a Sunday afternoon, we had an emergency meeting with her head nurse. She informed us that the only thing left in their arsenal to help Angie was a sedation drug typically used with surgeries. It isn't a drug used in the hospice setting very often, typically the wide variety of other narcotics are enough to keep pain and anxiety away. But they had never given any patient as much medication as they had Angie with virtually no effect in calming her pain or anxiety. Ang was once again a unique case. Only a couple other patients prior to Ang had needed to use this sedation drug, both were young people with cancer in their bones and sarcoma.

I immediately struggled, flashbacked to Conrad on the paralytic drug, his face getting red and tears squeezing from his shut eyes, rolling down his cheeks, crying without making a noise or a movement.

I knew how much pain Ang was in. I knew this was her only hope for relief. I knew she could not handle more. I knew she just wanted it all to be over.

The nurse had asked Ang. She had explained to her that this new drug, given in dosages appropriate for the scenario, would make her more drowsy and less likely to wake. When she did stir, it would be difficult for her to talk but it would provide her more relief. Ang did not hesitate. In her pain-stricken state, she shook her head that she understood and that she wanted whatever would provide relief. The family agreed.

For the most part, it worked. It allowed her to finally rest again. When she did stir, it wasn't for as long but she still had episodes occasionally. Those last four days, although a little calmer, were just as impossible as the others. Impatiently waiting for something we didn't want to happen. We weren't ready to lose her yet could not wait for her to go all at once. We could not stand to see her in this condition any longer. This wasn't Ang, and this wasn't a way to live.

Cassy's Perspective

July 15, 2016, is a special day I will never forget as long as I live as at 11:36 am my sweet 9 lb. 1 oz. baby boy, Anson Ray, was born. It is a day I will always cherish and always celebrate. However, one year later, to the day, our parents called Jessy and me up to the hospice house as the nurses thought it may be Angie's last day. It was the day the doctor's pulled out the big guns and gave her sedation medication. They told us that even if Ang made it through the day, we may not ever get the chance to see her open her eyes or hear her talk to us again.

We celebrated Anson's first birthday in the dining hall of the hospice house, eating store-bought cupcakes in between quick, quiet visits back to Angie's room. Such an extremely different scenario than when my oldest turned one and we went all out, practically turning his first birthday into a national holiday. It was the most depressing day, as I knew my son would never remember his Aunt Ang. He'd never have a birthday picture with her or a card that read "Happy Birthday Anson! Love Aunt GiGi" like all the other nieces and nephews. I wasn't only mourning the loss of my sister, but the loss of my children's aunt.

Almost daily we got the same call, thinking today was the day we'd have to say our final goodbye. One night, shortly after Angie entered hospice, Mom called Jessy and I up and we had a "slumber party" in Angie's room. It was peaceful being able to spend time with Ang not having anyone else up there to share her with. I felt my heartstrings being pulled. I wasn't completely sure I'd be able to handle being with Ang when she took her final breaths, yet I felt not being there would be almost harder. Every time I left the room though, I knew she knew I loved her, that I was there for her. We all were.

Cassie's Perspective

Angie had been sleeping most of the time now for a few days, with help from the sedation medications. Occasionally she would briefly wake up to ask a question and always say I love you. Someone was always with her, never wanting her to wake up alone or even worse to die alone. Her breathing becoming more labored, the nurses were always on top of it making sure she was as comfortable as possible. Stopping by quietly, never intruding, but always letting us know they were near. So many people in the lobby still praying and sharing memories, doing puzzles for hours on end. I found out later my mother even spent a night on a couch in the lobby without me even being aware, just in case we needed her.

Dinner and supper were brought day after day, most of the time we never knew who our provider was but were always grateful. At the end of the long days, it was time for Jessy and Cassy to go home because despite what we are going thru inside, outside the world still goes on. Work to go to and children to be loved and fed. And again, they'd go home with a heavy heart, knowing very well it easily could be the last time they would see their sister alive.

On July 20, a couple hours after Jessy and Cassy left, Angie's breathing became more and more difficult, the nurses still helping her in every way they knew how. I sang old familiar songs, talked to her, and most of all watched her face continuously for signs of stress. We promised her that she would not die with that terrifying feeling of being unable to breathe. This time her face was calm and peaceful. Her breathing was getting worse but this time she didn't seem to be aware.

I prayed hard and somewhat loud. I prayed not for her to be spared, even though that is what I wanted. Instead, I prayed, "Lord, you said if we followed you that you would go ahead and prepare a room in Your house. You promised." I prayed that God would take her suffering away and bring her peace like the home we know on earth. I prayed, "Jesus, you died a horrible death on the cross so we would have a home with you......You promised."

At 11:45 on July 20, Angie took her last breath, and she was peaceful. And we were heartbroken, in pain beyond any other pain I have ever known. I wanted to take it all back. I wanted her back without the suffering.

The nurse and Russ and I listened to the song *Jealous of the Angels,* a song I heard for the first time earlier that afternoon and it was perfect because I was so jealous of the angels and everyone else that was with Angie, already in Heaven.

The nurse gave us some time to say our goodbyes and let family know. Then she came back in and we had a ceremony right at Angie's bedside. It was beautiful, peaceful and uninterrupted with no distractions.

On our way home, early in the morning, Russ and I dug deep to find the positives of having our 26-year-old daughter die. We knew if we didn't focus on the positives this would rip our lives apart. We are thankful she didn't suffer for years and that we were given four months to continue to show her how much she made a difference and how much we loved her. We are thankful that we know where she is and that she wasn't missing somewhere. We reminded ourselves while 26 is young, it is more years than some people are given to say goodbye. And while she was doing so many beautiful things on earth, Jesus was only 33-years-old, and He was saving the world. Time is a human measurement, not a God one. It was on our way home that we decided we wanted to throw a party in Angie's honor for all her friends that held her hand by texting, calling, praying, laughing and loving her to the very end.

That night, it rained the most beautiful rain. It was not in the forecast but desperately needed by the farmers after several dry weeks. It was a God Thing, giving us what we needed, and we were thankful. The rain was tears of happiness at her entering Heaven's gate and tears of sorrow here on earth for all the dark days ahead without her.

CHAPTER 24

Entering Heaven's Gates

CARINGBRIDGE POST
by Jessy Paulson, July 21, 2017

On Thursday, July 20 at 11:45 pm, Angie earned her wings.
A Funeral Service for Angela Marcy Hazel will be held at 10:00
a.m. Monday, July 24th at the Hudson Lutheran Church in Hudson,
South Dakota, Burial will follow in the Grace Hill Cemetery a
with a luncheon to follow.

Cinters Perspective

In early summer, Angie and I talked about tattoos. Now, I have
never been a tattoo person. They were ok to me if it had a personal
meaning but otherwise I could do without. Angie had told me she
wanted to get another tattoo. A few years prior, all three girls had
gotten matching sister tattoos.

I asked her what she was thinking, and she took out a post-it note
and made a drawing of a cross and Faith Over Fear. I told her I
wasn't sure if she could get one now with her immune system so
low but that we could discuss with her doctor if it was important to
her. The next time we saw the doctor we asked, and he said that was
fine, but she should probably wait until her numbers were better.
Angie never had the chance to get the tattoo but now after she
passed, I knew I wanted it as soon as possible.

When others heard about it, it kind of exploded. My niece, who
was 17 at the time and visiting Florida in June was the first to get

---

the tattoo Angie drew. Cassy, Jessy and Kyle each got their own version of the Faith Over Fear tattoo. Of course, John had already gotten his beautiful tribute tattoo, in true loving fashion, outdoing everyone else's. In total there were at least a dozen of us who got tattoos with Angie's mantra, Faith Over Fear, to have a constant reminder as we went through the rest of our life without her.

It was time to make the arrangements for her services. I can't remember exactly when, but one day during the spring, Angie told me she was picking out the dress she would be buried in. In fact, she had a dress in her online cart from a boutique that she had been thinking about buying for a while, but thought it was a little too much money. I remember her telling me that a mother shouldn't have to pick out the dress that her daughter gets buried in. I had teased her that she just didn't want me to pick out her clothes, that she was afraid I would pick out something hideous. She ordered the dress and it was delivered to our house. But, at the time when we needed it, the dress was nowhere to be found. Angie had taken it back to Kansas City at some point and her closest friend found it for us there. Angie picking out the dress so we didn't have to was just another example of how selfless she was, always putting the other person first.

John's Perspective

On July 20th, 2017 we handed off our duty and now it's time to focus on doing what Angie would have been doing for others. So where does that leave us? What does it all mean? Answers we continually seek, and this is part of a process that ultimately helps us grow. I feel that my takeaways are to always try and be appreciative of your support team and family, be helpful in an ongoing way, and to be bold and unafraid of doing things you feel is appropriate. I was in a way lucky to be a part of something special; people relying on other people in a selfless manner, I was fortunate to see this in such a big way in a place that we are constantly barraged with negative news, stories, and content in general.

Angie will be missed by many, myself no different. She made a huge impact in my life and I witnessed her have a positive impact on so many others, that it's inspiring. I hope at the end of all this, that's how she will be remembered and how she will continually impact this world now that she is gone.

Jenny's Perspective

After Angie entered the gates of Heaven, I felt broken-hearted relief. She was finally pain free and I know without a doubt she was welcomed with open arms by Grandpa and so many other loved ones. But here we were. Sad. Upset. Completely broken-hearted.

The days after her death were filled with planning and so many people. Neighbors and friends, family from near and far, and even complete strangers stopped by our houses at all hours dropping off food and offering a hug. So many people, some had been a part of our lives forever, others just joining as part of Team Angie. All there to offer love and support.

And then suddenly there were others that became part of the story that caught me off guard. *So many others* that had been silently supporting Angie and our family throughout her battle. These were the people that were quietly praying the hardest through it all. The people who truly knew what Angie and our family was up against these last four months, because they too had been down this road and experienced a tremendous loss. These people had been here all along, hidden behind the loud cheers of Team Angie. Still part of the team but waiting on the bench, hoping they would never be needed. And now, here they were. These were the people that knew exactly what to say, or exactly what not to say in some cases. They were the people that could sum up how we felt and comfort us with just one look. Every time we ran across someone from this club, it was a God Thing. These people quickly became our refuge from those who, while with good intentions, just did not understand.

Entering Heaven's Gates

We knew that Angie's story had a wide impact on our community, on her circle and beyond but we didn't start truly comprehending just how large of an impact she had until the day of her prayer service. The receiving line to offer condolences for our family was unbelievably long and we were constantly surprised by those who traveled the distance to attend. A couple car loads of Angie's co-workers arrived, traveling hours from Kansas City to Hudson. Unbelievable, as she hadn't been working since she was diagnosed. Family and friends of Angie's and John's, from all over the country arrived. All of them stopping everything to be there, to celebrate the life of this amazing woman.

After the prayer service, my parents invited Angie and John's friends back to the farm to share stories. It was a combination of Angie's friends throughout her life. Friends who she had known since childhood; the kids that she went to preschool with and graduated from high school with. Those were the friends who knew all her deepest, darkest secrets and most humiliating stories because they were right there with her through it all. Those were the friends who had sleepovers at this same house and ran on this same farm through the mud playing, make-believe games. Joining them, were the friends Angie gained during and since college, many through John and their life in Kansas City. Those were the friends who became like a second family, the ones she traveled with, learned from, and became an adult with.

Sitting back at that gathering, I got teary-eyed as I saw these people interact. It was the most gorgeous melting pot of who Angie was. Everyone from different walks of life, all there because of Angie. Those who she gained as friends later had never been to Angie's hometown, never to the farm where she was raised. Many of them were city kids, amazed that this place was where Angie grew up. They thought they knew Angie well, but were surprised to constantly find out more about her. As I walked through the crowd I heard, "Wow, this is exactly what I hope to give my kids someday. A quiet place in the country to run around." "Look at this, it's beautiful and so peaceful here. This is where Angie was raised? No wonder she was so down to earth." A million stories of,

"Remember when" added to the conversation as seeing the farm sparked different memories for the ones that grew up with Angie.

In the middle of it all were kids running around, all of Angie's nieces and nephews along with kids of friends and family. At one point, Aleigha and Charley decided to organize a talent show with the other kids. In true Angie fashion, they demanded the attention of everyone to show their talents. In that moment, all of these people who had just met these kids, all of those friends who had traveled long distances, most without children of their own, stopped their conversation and gathered around the kids to cheer them on. Ang would've been so proud. Proud to see her nieces and nephews carry on her enthusiasm and theatrics and proud of her friends who made these kids feel so special in such a rough time. It was clear she attracted people as thoughtful and good-hearted as she was.

The whole night was such a testament of the kindhearted, friendly, energetic soul that Angie was. An absolute celebration of her life.

Angie's tribe at her Celebration of Life party at the farm.

Carter's Perspective

Here we are having a party just a couple days after our beautiful baby girl died. Were we crazy? It was a party to celebrate her love for everyone and to show our appreciation to all of her friends that stopped their lives to be with Angie as she started her new one.

I honestly don't really remember talking to anyone more than just small talk. *Hi. Thanks for coming. Do you need anything?* Then on to the next person, never pausing for too long knowing that would just start the tears flowing again, but I was so grateful for everyone there.

CHAPTER 25

Multiplying Memories

CARINGBRIDGE POST
by John Kolbach, July 31, 2017

Angie's eulogy as given by her fiancé John:

When I first met Angie I was instantly attracted to her. She had a glow about her paired with an infectious smile. After our first night of hanging out, I wanted Angie's number but my phone was dead. Instead of finding a bar napkin or another traditional method of getting her number, she instead grabbed a pen and my arm. She wrote her number over the entirety of my forearm and told me I better not shower if I wanted to ever get ahold of her again. She gave me a hard time about that night, and how many times I repeated myself, saying that she had beautiful eyes.

As we continued our relationship I got to know more and more about her. She was just as beautiful person on the inside as she was on the outside. She always put other people before herself, worried about little things that other people otherwise wouldn't even recognize, and always genuinely cared about people.

I always thought of myself as a tough individual, a strong person. It wasn't until this year that I learned what both of those terms truly meant. Tough is when you have to make countless visits to a doctor, for another appointment you didn't want to make. To walk into a hospital and wait to hear news that will determine your fate as a human being. Strong is putting on a smile every day, no matter how difficult. To appear and make people believe you are fine when internally you are not. As Angie fought her fight, I saw the same person that made her such a great individual; she was a caring, loving and a selfless person. I'm proud of her in a way she wasn't even willing to recognize. She was polite to every caring professional, often times flashing her contagious smile. During treatments, it was easy to see that the nurses were eager to visit and check on Angie. After any first visit, a name badge was no longer necessary. Angie would remember not only their name but carry on the last conversation they had together. "How was your vacation last week?" "Let's see it's been a few weeks since I've seen you now, 14 weeks along right?" She has always been sharp with recalling those details, and that never failed her!

It's easy to ask 'why' in these types of situations, but I can guarantee that many times questions that start with 'why' don't always offer a logical answer. Instead I urge everyone to remind themselves not the why's but the 'who.' Who Angie was; a caring, passionate, smart, loving, witty, and yes even a funny person! Angie flashed humor even in her final weeks of care. For instance, on one particular hot and humid Sioux Falls day, Russ asked Anita for the keys because he wanted to make sure the laptop wasn't going to get damaged in the heat inside of the car. Without a chance for Anita to answer or even hand over the keys, Angie boldly interjected, "Hey don't even think about it Dad!" As the room looked at Angie puzzled, she returned her stare and casually responded, "He's only wanting the keys to get himself licorice!" Not 5 minutes later when I left the room and walked down the hallway did I see Russ, eating a handful of licorice in the lobby by himself! Nothing got by her!

When we initially started dating during a road trip, I had said something that got Angie to laugh. Not too long after did I realized she was still staring at me in a way that I knew she was in some sort of deep thought. As I asked her what she was thinking about and she responded, "You know in past relationships I'm usually the funny one. I'm not too sure how I feel about this!" since that time I've done my best to convince all of our friends that yes she is indeed the funny one of the group!

It's also easy in these situations to acknowledge Angie was taken far too soon with plenty still to offer. At 26 years old a person should be thinking of things related to their career, relationships, and preparing for a family of their own. It is unfortunate for anyone to instead be learning about medication names, tolerance levels, and side effects when they are stacked together. I would challenge anyone who is faced with that scenario to not focus on 26 and the shortness of life based around that number. But rather 26 multiplied by the people that knew her for the time she was with us. Her 2 older sisters, mother, and father; add that up and you have 104 years of memories. Just down the road an uncle and grandparents, combining for another 77 years of memories and time spent together. Nieces, nephews, grandparents, uncles, aunts, in-laws, and additional friends and family, years too many to count. Her impact will forever affect many people in many positive ways years beyond her time here. I was fortunate enough to know Angie for the past 5 years and thankful to be granted the additional time to ensure I expressed my feelings to her.

In a way we were all very lucky to have our final time with Angie, which allowed us to come to terms with things and let her know how truly loved she is and how missed she will always be! Russ and Anita you raised an amazing daughter, one you should be incredibly proud to speak about. Jessy and Cassandra, please know that Angie looked up to both of you as sisters and mothers.

Because Angie was such an amazing person she will be greatly missed, but because of those attributes she possessed, she will also bring great joy in memories we share as we reflect on who Angie was. It is now our job to live our lives the way Angie lived hers, to love without restrictions, to help any person in need, and to care for every person we pass.

Jenny's Perspective

The church and all the overflow rooms were packed for Angie's funeral. The streets around the church were lined with cars and firetrucks that were prepared to lead the funeral procession as a nod of respect to my Dad, a lifetime volunteer fireman in the community.

The room where family gathers for a prayer prior to the services was also full, and so hot. It was not air-conditioned and we could not have fit any more people into it. Following tradition, our family filed into the church as one group, led by John, Mom and Dad, Cassy and I and our families, followed by the grandparents, aunts and uncles, cousins and extended family. This group alone took up a quarter of the church.

During the funeral, my son started getting restless. I remember so vividly once again being torn between just wanting to sit and be Angie's sister and the responsibilities of the real world in taking care of my babies who needed me. My son, although three years old at the time and plenty big to sit still for church, got anxious and uncomfortable with all the crying around him. He didn't understand and was scared so he started to act up. He clung to me yet was causing a commotion that was interrupting those around who were quietly listening and grieving.

I picked him up, walked him from the front of the church to the back to bring him to the nursery, which in our small-town church is just a little closet of a room with a window and speaker, not staffed. I sat in there with him for a few minutes, tears streaming down my face trying to figure out what to do. One of the ushers, also a Dad, saw me struggling and took Conrad outside to see the fire trucks. An act of kindness that will never be forgotten.

When the services were over, everyone filed out of the church to their vehicles to begin the 10-mile drive to the cemetery. Angie would be laid down to rest in the spot next to Grandpa. While the sentiment was nice, all that kept popping into my head was that spot skipped a generation and should've never been for her.

As we drove along the country highways to the next town over, we went past the ethanol plant where my Dad works. There standing at the entrance was a handful of employees, hard hats held over their chests, giving their respects for the daughter of the man they had worked side by side with for years. They knew first-hand the struggle, they had been present for so much of Angie's childhood, seeing her play in games and sing in concerts alongside their own kids, following photos of her as she hit each milestone after graduation as my Dad showed off, proud as can be. They knew the number of days Dad had to leave work for an emergency, they saw the toll her illness took on him personally. As fathers and mothers, coworkers and friends, they felt the loss we were all feeling. The image of those people paying their respects will forever be burned in my mind. An unspoken gesture of respect to Angie and our Dad.

She is Gone

You can shed tears that she is gone, or you can smile because she has lived.

You can close your eyes and pray that she will come back or you can open your eyes and see all that she has left.

Your heart can be empty because you can't see her, or you can be full of the love that you shared.

You can turn your back on tomorrow and live yesterday, or you can be happy for tomorrow because of yesterday. You can remember her and only that she is gone, or you can cherish her memory and let it live on.

You can cry and close your mind, be empty and turn your back, or you can do what she would want: smile, open your eyes, love and go on.

-Unknown

CHAPTER 26

Thank You For The Love

CARINGBRIDGE POST
by Russ and Anita Hazel, July 31, 2017

I want all of you that have followed Angie's story on CaringBridge or on Facebook and those of you that have messaged, texted, called, or written to know that your prayers and words have meant everything to us. We didn't always respond because it was so overwhelming, but we did feel your endless support and love. Thank you for that.

I want to share a couple of stories with you, if you have already heard them, please bear with me. I don't want anyone to focus on the "why", because "why not?" As I have told many people we love Angie and never wanted her to go, but we have to remember she was a gift from God, and God made her so why WOULDN'T He want her back? Also, yes, she was only 26 years old, but our time is not the same as God's time, remember Jesus was only 33 years old. It is not about how long we live on earth, but rather what we do with our time here.

Some of you may have heard the stories about the angels. For those of you that haven't, I feel compelled to share these stories with you. On three different occasions and places throughout her life, Angie was allowed a glimpse that most of us will never get the privilege to experience.

One day, at the hospice house, Angie woke up while I was sitting beside her. Angie said, as calmly as can be, said she saw angels. I asked her what they were doing and she said, "just checking on me".

Another time before that, at the hospital, she told me she felt Jesus' hand on her shoulder. Nothing else, just His presence.

Then, there was one other time clear back when she was only 3 or 4 years old, at our church in Hudson. During the service she said she could see an angel in the front of the church. I asked her, "what does the angel look like?" She said she couldn't tell because she could only see the back of the angel and that she had long hair and wore something long and white, kind of like a dress. I know some people may say she was only 3 or 4 and how do you know? But, it wasn't just what she said, it was how she said it, and how she acted. She was very calm and not at all scared and I don't know how to explain it except to say it was a mother's intuition. She was not telling a story. I remember it was around Thanksgiving but there was no mention of angels in the readings or gospel that day.

I'm telling you this, so you know as much as we love her and miss her and although we will miss her forever, she truly is home now. I don't believe we are done hearing from her but we have to be open to it and quiet, so we can tell when she is close by.

The absolute best way to keep Angie alive in our hearts is to be like her. Take the extra step to be nice to your neighbor. Show unconditional love to those around you and Angie will live forever in our hearts.

CHAPTER 27

Why?

As posted on Facebook

Jessy Paulson
July 24, 2017 · 🌐 ▾

Today we celebrated the life of my sister. Today was by far one of the hardest days of my life and for many of you, I know it was also up there on your list of bad days too. But, reflecting back on today and reading some of the comments and sympathies sent our way over the last few days, I am troubled by something. So many are asking "why?". So many are saying they "don't understand".

Believe me, I get it. Back in March when Ang was first diagnosed, I was irate. I didn't know why. I wanted to by a f#<% cancer shirt for everyday of the week. I was mad at God and did not understand. But, as the events of the last few months went on, I discovered the why.

I know without a doubt this cancer, and the pain and suffering it caused, was inflicted by Satan. In fact, during the last few weeks of her life Ang would often say when the doubts and fears and anxiety crept in that it was Satan trying to steal her peace. And she was right. Satan caused this, but God used this to create good.

Lives needed to be changed, people needed to be inspired and God started using Angie to fulfill His purposes. Ang has always been this ray of sunshine, attracting friends and leaving an impact on people her entire life. God gave her that infectious smile, her contagious laugh, her incredible people skills and way with words. He molded her for His purpose. Over the last 4 months, I have been witness to the incredible service Ang was called to. She was changing lives of not only her friends and family but also people she had never met, with her strength, kindness, and faith. She was healing old wounds, providing hope, and drawing people to God. So, why Angie? Well, because of YOU, and me, and the 400+ people that showed up to her funeral today, and the 300+ that showed up at the prayer service last night, and the 35,000+ visits to the CaringBridge site. If it would've been some bum, we wouldn't have cared as deeply as we do. God used Angie's trials to bring ALL of us closer to Him. I could not be more proud of my sister for the life she has lived.

Today we are sad, but it is sadness for us, not for her. She was ready. She is living in Heaven for eternity because she was called and served God in a tremendous way at a magnitude many of us will never see.

So, if you are still asking why, go read her CaringBridge journal again. Read the comments and guestbook, read her Facebook wall, see the impact she has made. Don't let Satan steal your peace. Go on spread her message, live your life to the fullest and make Ang proud. That's exactly what we intend on doing.

Faith Over Fear.

CHAPTER 28

One Year Later

Cinters Perspective

This last year has been like a roller coaster. Up when we have been doing something constructive in Angie's name. Down when the grief slaps you in the face over and over. Does it get easier? I hesitate to say that, it is more like it allows you to catch your breath once in a while.

Immediately after Angie died, on the way home that night, Russ and I talked about how this hurt more than anything ever before in our lives. But we also talked about how this could have been so much worse. How some people seem to suffer for years and how some people are not given any time to say goodbye. We were given four months. We talked about how we knew Angie was strong in her faith and without a doubt now in Heaven with our Lord. We reminded ourselves that when God gives you a child to take care of they are a gift, the child is not permanently yours. They are a gift until they need to go home.

We drove into our driveway about 3 am that night. Getting up in the morning, life kicks you in the rear to get going, now is the time to make plans, mourn later. No time to grieve. We went to the funeral home to make arrangements. Thankful once again, God put people in our paths that we knew to help us and have the patience and compassion to do this job daily. Once the arrangements were made, we shifted gears to plan a party to show all of Angie's and John's friends how much we appreciated them. I wanted to do the party at the farm where our girls grew up.

Every day was busy sunup to sundown. I was so frantic to get Angie's home videos on DVD, to get all my favorite pictures of her hung up on the wall, to choose her stone, get her handwriting stamped on a custom piece of jewelry I could wear daily, to get the memory garden in our yard created. Always trying to make everything into something physical that I could hold or look at anytime and anywhere I wanted.

Then it was like the rollercoaster crashed down the hill. I went back to work at the library only a week after she had passed, feeling as if I had relied on my co-workers far too long already. I went back to babysitting the grandkids within a month after she passed as they were starting school and needed some consistency in their lives, too. I remember thinking this is not enough time to grieve and, honestly, I had it the best out of all of us. Russ and the girls had to go back to work almost immediately. I was angry thinking of that. A mother has 6-12 weeks when a child is born, as they should, to bond, but there is no such time frame when a child dies. I know there is a fine line between the time to grieve and the time to get back to the real world, but 3-5 days doesn't seem like enough. I can't imagine anyone's work is their best. Especially considering one thing that really sticks out is how forgetful we all became right after. I couldn't remember anything. I thank God for his guidance and keeping us all safe during this state of mind. My heart hurt for Jessy and Cassy as their lives had to move on without a chance to grieve.

The roller coaster peaked whenever we had a chance to do something good in Angie's name. She told us at one point she didn't want a park bench with her name on it. She wanted to make a difference. I focused on that often.

Before school started, I took my granddaughters, Aleigha and Charley, shopping for the Backpack Program, a local program that provides food for school-age kids to take home if they need it. It was a program that really spoke to Angie and her life work. We had a wonderful time trying to pick healthy choices that Angie would have approved of, but also remembering that Angie said you can eat anything you want in moderation. We cried but it was a good cry because once again God was showing us people who needed a little extra lift and giving us an outlet to continue her work.

Despite constantly looking for the good and holding on as tight as I could, I fought with myself every hour. I wanted nothing more than to wallow in my own self-pity, get drunk and smoke until I couldn't cry anymore. But I continued my fight with the devil, determined to see all the good things. Life was a rollercoaster.

I didn't sleep, at most 2 hours at a time. Most nights I spent listening to music. *I Can Only Imagine* became my go-to song to help me see Angie in Heaven. I'd watch You-Tube videos that Angie shared with me, specifically one about a husband giving a eulogy at his wife's funeral who died of cancer. Anything to keep my focus on God and finding peace.

In September, Russ and I, Jessy and Kyle and Cassy went to John and Angie's house in Kansas City to help John go through Angie's personal belongings. Once again, it was like a roller coaster up and down, and at times upside down, smiling and crying all at once from all the memories. Pulling up to the driveway stole my breath away, expecting to see her come out of the house to give one of her never ending hugs. Expecting to see her in the kitchen making some new healthy-but-still-has-meat-in-it-recipe that would get Russ and Kyle's approval. Everything was just like it was the last time we were there, like she ran to the grocery store because she forgot something. That is, until I went downstairs, and the flashbacks began of her sitting on the couch feet up under a blanket coughing constantly, unable to get up on her own or when I went into her bedroom and saw everything still in place, more flashbacks of laying by her to help her in the middle of the night.

That evening after a really hard day of going through things, we sat outside by the fire. I thought here is my chance to sit back and enjoy a drink and a chance to have a smoke. Well anyone who knows me knows that I rarely drink anymore, so that didn't last long. Even though I quit years ago, I tried a smoke and again they tasted terrible. I quickly realized that neither was going to help, it would only make things worse tomorrow. Our trip was hard and made even harder when we left knowing we would probably never be back. Watching all of Angie's and John's dreams together disappear as we drove away from the cul-de-sac.

I wanted to get her headstone picked out quickly, so it could be up as soon as possible. Russ suggested we go to the same place they went for his Dad's headstone, the year before as they had done a nice job. I called them and explained I was looking for a different shaped stone, I knew I wanted a heart or something. They were unable to help me that day. A couple days later I drove past a memorial stone place that had a heart one outside and stopped and looked. It was nice but still not exactly what I wanted. Then the following day, a salesman from a different company called me, told me their name and who they worked for and it was a family business. Normally I would've blown them off thinking they were ambulance chasers but the tone of his voice and the compassion he showed made me pause and listen. When I asked what he had for uniquely shaped headstones, he went on to describe a teardrop and I knew in my heart that was it. A couple months after everything was done, I saw a TV commercial for the company that stated a portion of their sales goes to Feeding South Dakota. That is when I knew that phone call was a God Thing and Angie was guiding me to the perfect stone.

Visiting Angie's place at the cemetery was always a mix of emotion. Crashing down the rollercoaster when I pulled in and slowly trekking back up the hill when time after time I would find something someone left there in remembrance of Angie and it would lift my spirit. I never knew who left all those things.

I spent a lot of time focusing on building our own memory garden at the farm, full of flowers and many other things that remind us of Angie. Something we can add to every year. I adore the windchimes that hang in it and feel her nearby whenever they chime.

In early fall, we went to Illinois to deliver Angie's car to one of my nieces, and it felt so good that someone who knew and loved Angie would also love her car as much as she did when she bought it.

We went back to KC to a celebration of life given by her co-workers. This wonderful group of friends who gave a piece of their heart every day to help others were part of Angie's family in KC and we are so blessed to have gotten to know them. They helped Angie every day by all their messages, prayers and everything else they did. What a blessing our world would have if everyone had coworkers like those people.

Soon, the holidays were upon us, and we were trying to keep it together for the grandkids. I never thought I should hide every tear from them. They needed to know it was ok to cry and that it was ok to be sad and miss Angie and talk about her. But on the other hand, I didn't want to scare them or make them feel as if they couldn't talk about her because it might make us cry. I wanted them to understand she was in the best place and I was crying simply because I missed her.

In the meantime, two beautiful babies were born miles apart from each other but held together by one common bond. One is John's niece, Adalynn Hazel. The other is the daughter of friends of Angie and John's, Hayden Faith. They both have part of Angie with them in their parent's love for Angie and in their names. Thank you to their parents for the legacy of Angie to live on in your children. What a tremendous gift you have shared with all of us.

April 5th, Angie's birthday, I planned for months. I desperately did not want the day to pass by with only a muttering of "Today would've been Angie's 27th birthday." So, Russ and I, Jessy, Cassy, and Aleigha skipped out of school and work early and went to Omaha to a Mercy Me Concert. We were then back to the top of the roller coaster celebrating our baby's birthday with our family. It was fantastic.

In May, we participated in a Walk to Remember, put together by a local ministry run by another family who had lost a child. It was bittersweet and full of tears to be together with so many other parents who have had to give up their children so much sooner than they were prepared to. We didn't walk in the same shoes as every story is unique but definitely walked the same path.

By summer, we were invited to go to Rosebud Reservation to deliver backpacks and other items with our church. Russ and I decided to go for the day, not dreaming how much it would impact our lives. We attended a church service filled with kids and adults from our community mixed with people from the Rosebud community. The leaders of the Rosebud community led the service, and, toward the end of it, they shared their story of how they also had a daughter who went to live with the Lord sooner than her parents were expecting. It was their heartbreaking story that led to many of our own flashbacks of Angie's trials. During the service, they asked us to come to the front. Totally and completely out of mine and Russ' comfort zone. These people, who at the beginning of the day were strangers, now were sharing their story and love for God with us, praying and crying for us and all the adults from our community also praying and crying with us. It was thru this that once again we realized how truly blessed we are and God is with us every step of the way.

I still selfishly grieve for the future. The wedding where her Dad will never be able to walk her down the aisle, the grandchildren with her beautiful smile who we will never meet. Our family pictures will always have an empty place. I miss Angie every hour of every day. She is our baby girl who always made everyone feel like home.

Cassy's Perspective

Looking down at my once again round belly, I am reminded that life keeps moving on, whether you are ready for it or not. It reminds me of the milestones and the moments Angie is missing here on Earth even though we all wish we could hit a pause button and just breathe in her memory and absorb the loss we've suffered.

Most of the time I feel like Angie is just away, either down in

Kansas City or maybe on vacation. I miss her terribly, but I will see her again. It makes getting through the day slightly easier. Then out of the blue something will trigger my senses and I realize that no, that's not true. She's gone–gone, gone. And the permanency hits like a huge wave, making me lose my footing and I get swept away in my grief.

When Angie passed, my boys were so young that having any sort of concept of death was almost impossible. My inquisitive Haizen had so many questions just trying to wrap his little 3-year-old brain around what happened to his Aunt Gigi and why his mommy was always so sad. I remember one day on our way to the babysitter's he asked, "Mama, is there a floor in Heaven?" Instantly I began to wonder where this conversation was going and I asked him what he meant. Haizen replied, "If there is a floor in Heaven how does Angie see or hear us? You said she can." He must not have gotten a clear enough answer from me because a couple days later he went to my Mom and asked her the same thing trying to grasp an answer he could understand.

Bedtime is when the questions come out the most though. I've kept on the tradition our Mom started with Jessy, Angie and I and snuggle in bed with our boys until they fall asleep, lots of times falling asleep in bed with them myself. It's fifteen minutes or so we get to spend together without any interruptions when they can fully relax and feel the warmth and comfort that only a parent can give. It's how I want my boys to fall asleep each night, knowing they are safe and loved. Most nights as we say our bedtime prayers Angie's name gets brought up, sometimes through stories of what she was like when she was a little girl. Other times I get asked the hard questions like, "Does Angie still have legs? She has wings now, so why does she need both?" But lots of nights it's a tired, teary-eyed little boy coming to me saying how he misses Angie. All I can really offer is a hug, usually too choked up to say much more than, "I know buddy, so do I."

Anson, on the other hand, had only just turned one last July when we lost Angie so I do not get asked hard questions by him. That's hard, too, because he doesn't realize what he's missing. Unfortunately, he doesn't hold those precious memories the other nieces and nephews do. He will only know her through pictures and stories told by us of the beautiful aunt he has who lives in Heaven. One day last fall, I ran home from work for a lunch break and my Mom had been babysitting. There was my Mom in the rocking chair, Anson on her lap and holding her phone. "Show mama, who this is," my Mom said to Anson, proud that she had taught him something new. And clear as day he pointed to the picture on her phone and said "Gigi." It was the first time he said her name and it crushed me.

Now we have a new baby on its way, one Ang would be so excited about, the entire time praying for a girl. It's hard sometimes to be as happy about this pregnancy as the last two, knowing she will never get to hold this baby or rock it to sleep. Knowing she never got to feel a baby kick inside of her. Just admitting that makes me feel horrible because I know that I am blessed beyond belief to carry another child into this world. Hopefully one that has hair brighter than the sun or a child that knows how to march to the beat of their own drum. Just preferably not one that likes to bounce out of bed before 5:30 a.m. like Angie used to as a toddler.

The waves will always be there, no matter how many days, or weeks, or years go by. Our first Christmas hit me harder than the day of Angie's diagnosis or even her funeral. It pulled me under so hard and so unexpectedly that day and once again the Mom guilt overtook me along with the sadness of not having my sister with us to celebrate a holiday that meant so much to our family. The anxiety crept up as the morning went on, the boys ripping open gifts giving me flashbacks of 25 years ago when it was my sisters and I squealing in excitement that Santa had come. By the time we were ready to leave for my parents to celebrate I had locked myself in the bathroom unable to breathe, begging Zack and the boys to just give me a *minute*. I didn't want to fall apart in front of our boys and ruin their Christmas. It was so hard for my husband to understand why I was acting so irrational after months of holding myself together. I just couldn't. Life hurt. So I took a deep breath, got in the car and went to my parents to fall apart on my Mom instead. That's what moms are for, to be a place of comfort and warmth for their child.

Being Angie Hazel's older sister will always be one of my greatest honors. She fought her battle with such extreme strength and grace that it only could have come from God. I pray I will forever continue to be reminded to be positive, to spread her infectious personality in my actions, and have Faith Over Fear.

I now, like many others, have a tattoo in Angie's honor as a constant reminder of this. Though Angie did not receive a miraculous recovery like we had hoped, we did experience more miracles than we could count. For the last four months of her life we have all leaned on one another, grown closer to God and learned how much one life can impact so many others.

My prayers to God in the years to come are not that I have fewer waves that hit me, just that God continues to throw me a lifesaver when I feel myself going into uncharted waters. To know that he'll always be there to make sure I don't drown. Losing Angie has been heartbreaking, but each time I fear my feet are slipping I remember all of the amazing things that have happened in our family since Angie got sick. That these are God Things and to live by Angie's mantra the way she'd want me to by having Faith Over Fear.

John's Perspective

Upon the burial process, we released purple balloons. A small note, message, and option for anyone who would come across a downed balloon to read about Angie's story. All I could honestly think about was I wanted out of South Dakota, and to return to Kansas City. Not sure the primary driving force but it didn't matter at the time for me! In retrospect I still think about why. Running from a new reality? Ready to accept it? I don't know, and I suppose it still doesn't matter. What did matter is that whether I liked it or accepted it (or neither of those), I had to realize and adapt to something different. Everyday proved to be different to some degree, some days more difficult, others easier to process and build a positive perspective. The house once shared now seems bigger, most times quieter, and at very select times like a bit of a prison. A place filled with pictures and memories, constant reminders more or less.

A part of things for me since Angie's passing are when I have dreams with her included. While dreams can often be many things with wide-spectrum affairs, mine tend to usually be very realistic. Usually with friends or family, doing activities that aren't too far-fetched from previous experiences. At first, dreams always had Angie in her last physical state when she was sick. Slowly, it's transitioned to Angie looking like she did prior to when she was sick; long blonde hair, walking upright, and partaking in whichever event the dream allowed. My hopes are that, internally, I'm subconsciously remembering Angie for who she was, not just her last physical state. Maybe eventually when I have those dreams, she isn't even sick at all. My point with this topic isn't to describe my dreams in detail but to help people understand the impact these unavoidable experiences create in the mornings. That moment when you wake and things go from a dream state to reality, processing and reflecting on what just took place internally. Sometimes replaying those dreams in your head through your morning routine, or just the realness it can create that tap into and activate emotions.

Visiting back to South Dakota feels more comfortable each time I go back. After one particular trip, unable to see all the people I had hoped, I realized a new challenge was present. How do you spend your time and still try and see everyone you had hoped? I try not to disappoint, I genuinely want to see so many people that offered support along the way, but realizing that may not always be fulfilled. Visits to Angie's family without her feel just as comfortable, if not more comforting than one may expect. Throughout there are always a few things that surprise me, emotionally speaking. The first visit to where Angie was buried being one of the times that easily creeps into my head as I think and write it out. That may seem like a common place and experience that would trigger emotions but I just assumed that I'd arrive, experience those sensations, and exit once I felt collected.

Side note and a bit of a funny sub point, along that initial drive to Hawarden, IA (where Angie was laid to rest), without navigation I would be a liability on the road! It was always on the drives to her parents' house, one I've made plenty in the past 5 years, I still relied on her to navigate each turn. Long story short, there were many missed turns due to my lack of navigation, and her lack of attention at that point of the drive!

So back to the drive. I figured it would be at the site where I'd get the chance to figure out my emotions in that moment. What I didn't expect was that drive solo. One that made me think of all those "missed turns" memories. Additional memories quickly followed, ones that I didn't even recall until I passed them. Driving by the vet, the same vet we took Kona to when we first got him to get his 9-inch puppy nails clipped, etc. It was a scrapbook of memories I hadn't planned for. I view that scenario as an example of one of the very elementary perspectives an outsider wanting an insider glimpse can have. It seems like it's depicted in every movie, or maybe even understood at the human level, when you lose someone that first visit (or any visit) to the burial can be heavy. But I'd offer the perspective that there are moments prior, post, even unrelated; the ones you don't consciously notice that can trigger feelings, senses, and atmospheres you otherwise never detected.

My 'perspective' of my own loss is this: a loud, internal struggle, but one that isn't always externally noticeable. *What would that person I lost think of me now? Would they be proud of my actions? (And quite possibly) What would they be doing if they were in my position?* I can only hope that Angie would answer all of those questions in a positive manner toward me, but I do feel an internal weight to do her proud. I think that all those close to her have that same weight on their shoulders. There are moments that slowly create a body of work, and we are in a position to now look at Angie's body of work and be proud of how she fulfilled her moments from beginning to end. It's not hard to understand by looking at that, how one wouldn't have that strong urge to try and live up to those expectations.

Jenny's Perspective

When I get outside early enough in the mornings to see the sunrise, all I see is Ang in the sky. I feel her presence most at that time of day. The pinks and oranges gently lighting up the sky remind me of a day she spent at my kitchen table painting with my kids and I about a month before she passed away. That day she deliberately took her time mixing colors and gently brushing strokes of greens and blues on canvas, painting a succulent that now hangs in my house as a memory of one of the last real uninterrupted moments we had together. Cancer was not mentioned that day, it was just us.

I miss everything about Ang, but the biggest hole for me comes in the most unexpected times. When I'm flipping through a magazine and see a floral wallpaper that I know she would've loved, when I turn on the news and want to banter politics with someone and her and Grandpa are not there, when someone accidentally calls me by her name, when I see her name missing from the family group text, when I talk so fast others can't keep up but I know she would've understood every word, when I have a dumb joke or witty comment that no one else gets but it was exactly her sense of humor and she would've laughed.

Sometimes I can swallow the grief in the moment, refocus my thoughts and keep on with my day. Other days it feels like the grief swallows me whole and I don't have a fighting chance against it. Those are the days it's just hard. Those are the days that if it wasn't for my kids and my husband and work and my millions of projects, I could easily just curl up in a ball and cry all day.

For as long as I can remember my Mom has unknowingly prepared me for this and so many hard moments still to come in my life.

In the most loving way, our Mom taught us from a very young age that its OK to have overwhelming feelings of doubt, sadness, anxiety, and even fear. It is OK to let those feelings wash over you, but you need to learn how to swim in them, not sink. Anytime us girls would fall apart, she would let us cry on her shoulder and lend her ear. But after a few moments she would say, "OK. But look at everything you have going for you. Count your blessings. Despite all this, what are you grateful for?" And she was right, the list of what we had was always so much longer than the list of what we did not have, even in the toughest of times.

My Mom didn't have the easiest path growing up. She had a lot of reasons why she could've lived underwater in the overwhelming emotions, and for a while she did. But there was a point in her life that she decided she needed to learn how to swim. And from that point on, she consciously made a choice every day, sometimes every moment, to choose the positive. Because of that, she was able to pick herself up, to rebuild broken relationships with her parents, move on after miscarriages, become the amazing mother and grandma she is today, and be a support for so many other friends and family members as they went through their own struggles and grief.

Today, I still see Mom making that conscious decision every day to find the good. Some days the good is in the grandkids, Dad, Cassy and I, or a friend. Some days it's seeing Angie's story continue to unfold from Heaven. Some days are harder than others, but every day she is consciously making the same decision, that she will let the grief wash over her, but she will not live underwater.

Everyone says that the firsts are the hardest, but I don't see how the seconds or thirds or even forty-fifths will be any easier. I think you get used to treading water and you get stronger but there will still be a current that pulls you under every once in a while, no matter how long it has been.

Christmas was hard. The Blue Christmas Service at church, designed for those grieving, was hard because it was the first time since her funeral that I set foot in Hudson Lutheran. It was hard because my four-year-old, who gets uncomfortable when people cry, started raising chaos again. Hard because my daughter was sobbing next to me and I could not comfort her. Hard because my other daughter was quietly coloring a picture of "Angela the Angel" and I could see the hurt in her eyes. Hard because once again life was so chaotic it was difficult for me to even grieve.

Decorating the tree and seeing ornaments from my childhood sparked memories of us girls decorating the tree, Ang usually tiring of it halfway through and running off to play, only to show up again just in time for Dad to lift her up to put the angel on top.

Christmas shopping with my daughters led to Charley stopping in her tracks in the middle of Walmart to point out a ceramic elephant candle holder that "Angie would've loved." And she was right, it was totally Ang.

Yet despite how hard it was I made a conscious choice not to let it ruin my Christmas spirit. It has always been my favorite holiday and it was Angie's favorite too. Instead of crawling into a hole until the season was over, I instead took a note from my Grandmama, who *buried* her sister on Christmas Eve, forty-five years ago. Her sister, like mine, lost her battle to cancer at a young age. And what developed in the years after that was a huge Christmas Eve party at Grandmama's house each year. Grandmama turned what was undoubtedly one of her hardest days into one of the most joyous days of the year for me and my sisters and so many of our other family members.

Because of Grandmama's and Mom's strength and lifelong guidance, our family moved forward, may it be with tears in our eyes, to celebrate the birth of Jesus, the reason why Angie was able to celebrate her first Christmas in Heaven.

March brought another tough week. Every day reminding where life was a year ago when the bottom fell out from under Ang, from under us.

FAITH OVER FEAR

Amidst all the flashbacks and memories, I again tried to keep my faith at the forefront of my mind. As the dates showed up on the calendar marking one year since her diagnosis, since her first round of chemo, since the week from hell, I realized that the same week also marked four years since my son, Conrad, was taken off the ventilator and survived the rough battle with RSV that almost took his life. Instead of getting swallowed by the grief of the anniversary of Angie's diagnosis, I focused on the anniversary of blessings received that week, that Conrad survived, and that Angie was given the gift of more time.

One year felt pretty much the same as one hour, one day, one month…I'm guessing that every year until I die will feel the same. Our lives will constantly ache for Angie to be physically here. But in between all those moments that unexpectedly crush us with grief for everything that should've been, we see with clarity that God granted Angie His Ultimate Promise.

I still feel the words I wrote on the day of her funeral, that what we feel is a sadness for us, not for her. Why should we be upset that Angie beat us to the finish line? Why be sad that she entered the Promised Land before we did? When we stop for a moment and take off our grief blinders we see that ultimately the anniversary of her death is a day of rejoicing because it is the day God opened His arms and welcomed Angie home.

She was given one of the worst possible diagnoses, without any clear plan or way to be healed. We knew from the beginning that it would take a divine intervention. And that is what was received, just in the most unexpected way. Instead of healing her, God held on to her and we watched Angie show the world what it looks like to have hope and faith and trust even in the most uncertain times. Her unwavering faith sparked hope in so many people as we have heard in story after story this last year. That was the purpose of her life, and now one year later, I can more clearly see the purpose of my life, to share Angie's story with the world until I can hug her again.

One Year Later

I wonder if Jesus ever looked at his disciples when they were doubting and going astray, smiled, and thought to himself, "They have no idea what they are about to do for My Kingdom."

And then I wonder if Jesus looks at me in my moments of sin and weakness, smiles and thinks to himself, "She has no idea what she is about to do for My Kingdom."

-Unknown

IN REFLECTION

Angie will always be remembered as the person who was the first to smile and say hi, the last to let go in a hug, the one you looked forward to seeing, if only for a minute. Her infectious smile and kind soul attracted so many.

Angie and our family were blessed beyond measure in support. Everything from large fundraisers bringing in money to help pay medical bills and expenses, to prayer chains where thousands were lifting up her name, requesting a miracle to save her. And while we are so incredibly thankful for the generosity of the big gestures, the small gestures meant just as much. The smile from a stranger, the unexpected hug, the random text that someone was thinking of us, the loss of sleep from the middle of the night prayers.

So how does one person rally the support of so many? Because Ang has always been the generous soul offering the smile, the hug, the words of encouragement, and the quiet prayers to others. Her hopeful spirit overflowed to those around her and when the tables were turned, and she was the one needing the encouragement, people gave it freely, as she had to them.

Thinking back to Ang's final days, and the hell she was put through, it is hard to understand why and to lose our faith in the same God she was directing people towards. But as we reflect, we realize that maybe her pain and suffering at the end was to not only help us all further understand the depth of the fight Ang was living but also how badly the devil fights God for us all each and every day. Throughout her storm, she did not lose sight of her Savior. She questioned Him, she pleaded for Him, but she did not lose sight of Him. We know without a doubt that He carried her through the storm.

So often, God places us in situations where we learn details or are introduced to people that give us a glimpse as to what our purpose in life is. If we pay attention, all these "God Things" eventually line up to guide us in the direction of God's plan for our lives. The God Things lead us to a path of how to serve Him. Angie had big plans for her life that did not include cancer and did not end at age 26. Just like so many of us, her plans were not the same as God's plans and she had the same reservations we all do of jumping into the unknown. Yet, every day she humbly showed us through her words and actions how to blindly trust God through the hardest of times. I pray that when Angie entered Heaven she saw the full picture of her purpose in life unfold, that she saw the tremendous impact she made on so many, that she understood how God has used her and is continuing to use her life at a magnitude that we will never fully comprehend while on earth.

We decided to share Angie's story and our perspectives, because of how real it is. All of us are fighting a battle, all of us are searching for our purpose in life, trying to find our path. All of us have the devil breathing down our neck, trying to steal our peace. We are all struggling. However, we learned from Angie how to have faith no matter what we face. We pray Angie's legacy continues to draw people to God and we pray that you will help us spread her message.

Faith Over Fear forever.

AUTHORS

Jessy

Jessy Paulson lives with her husband, Kyle, their three kids, Aleigha, Charleanna and Conrad in an old general store, converted to a residence near Hudson, SD. Jessy spends every free moment she has in her workshop painting and creating repurposed projects. After the death of Angie, she is now committed to living her life to the fullest and sharing Angie's story with the world.

Anita

Anita Hazel, Mom to three beautiful girls, lives on a farm near Hudson, SD with Russ, her husband of 35 years. Anita is blessed to babysit her five (almost 6) grandchildren daily and work in her local library at night.

John

John Kolbach was raised in South Dakota. He received his degree at South Dakota State University and is currently living in the Kansas City area. He has one older brother and sister, along with a younger sister; each one married with children of their own. Along the way, John has lived in various cities and states, meeting great people at each location. With many of his family and friends living great distances apart, John often finds himself in a constant state of traveling, and enjoying time spent with that very support group who helps keep him on his path throughout life.

Cassy

Cassandra (Cassy) DeBruin resides in Alcester, SD with her husband, Zack and two sons. Haizen, 4 years old, and Anson, 2 years old, are the light of her life. Cassy and Zack are also about to be blessed with baby number three in February. When not spending time with her family or working Cassy enjoys painting furniture for her, Jessy and Anita's occasional home decor store.

About The Authors

Left to Right: Angie, Cassy, Jessy, & Anita

John & Angie

Made in the USA
Middletown, DE
04 November 2018